SEEING FRANCE

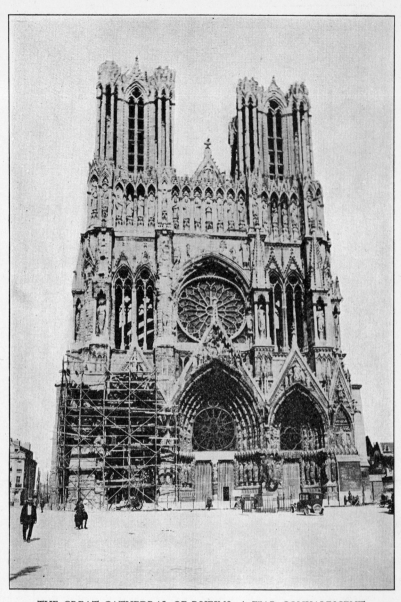

THE GREAT CATHEDRAL OF RHEIMS: A WAR CONVALESCENT

SEEING FRANCE

By

E. M. NEWMAN

Author of "Seeing Italy," "Seeing Russia," "Seeing Egypt
and the Holy Land," "Seeing Germany," "Seeing England
and Scotland," "Seeing Spain and Morocco," etc.

OVER 300 ILLUSTRATIONS
FROM ORIGINAL PHOTOGRAPHS

FUNK & WAGNALLS COMPANY
NEW YORK *and* LONDON
1930

INTRODUCTION

PARIS and its suburbs are omitted from this volume, because they are so rich in interest that they must, in due time, have a volume all to themselves. The title, "Seeing France," therefore, means seeing the chief attractions of France outside of the Ville Lumière.

In a travel-book such as this the author is usually expected to answer the oft-asked query, "Which do you consider the most interesting part of France?" Some readers may be disappointed when they do not find here a definite expression of opinion on that point. To my mind, however, it is not the author's province to pick and choose for his readers. There may be various reasons for writing fiction, but there should be only one excuse for a book of travels, and obviously that should be to present in a comprehensive way the places of interest—the scenic beauties, the art, architecture, life, customs, history and folklore of the country described—and let the reader's taste decide which cities and scenes are most likely to interest him.

Many a travel-writer has brought censure upon his head by failing to show a due appreciation of beautiful art and architecture. Others have been severely criticized because they paid too much attention to the frivolous side of a nation's life, to its doings after dark, overlooking or giving scant recognition to the more refining influences of what should be seen during the daylight hours. I have tried to avoid these causes of discontent on the part of the reader.

Paris may give a stranger a wrong impression of France. It constitutes a different world from the rest of the Republic. One cannot travel far outside of the French capital without coming into contact with a more serious phase of life. History has crept into every nook and corner. Religion sways the people to a marked degree, as seen in Pardons, Festivals and unusual processions, all of which form a dominating and integral part of the life of the peasants.

Historic châteaux beckon visitors in great numbers to the valley of the Loire. Mineral springs with curative properties become magnets for those in search of health. Lovers of nature find charm, grandeur, and majesty in the Alps or the Pyrenees, while the smart set seek such fashionable resorts as Deauville, Biarritz and Nice to display their gowns and jewels.

What appeals to one might offer little of interest to another. Assuming that an author is human in his likes and dislikes, his opinion is, after all, but the expression of an individual whose conclusions are subject to the same limitations as are those of any other man. For this reason it seems a wise precaution for a travel-writer to maintain a neutral attitude and to present the essential features and places of interest without showing a preference except in a general way.

Many people are tired of books and plays that deal with the World War; others for personal reasons find in the war zone more that appeals to them than anything else in France. To the average reader, I think, the former "front" has to-day only a historic interest, and for this reason I have not commented on it, but merely suggest what may be included in a visit to the former theater of war.

Would you have me contrast the merits of France with those of Italy, Germany or England? It would be futile. One might as well argue the relative qualities of four great composers: there would be a divergence of opinion on them even among musicians. We all discover things in one country that we do not find in another, and our interest depends naturally on our individual taste. Our familiarity with a language might influence our judgment in favor of one country and against another whose speech we do not understand.

"How long should I take to cover France?" That question has been repeatedly asked of me. As well inquire how long a foreigner should spend in the United States. It would depend on what he wanted to see and how much time he had at his disposal. Personally I think at least three or four weeks should be allowed for a tour of France, exclusive of the time spent in Paris; even then one should not expect to see everything of prime importance. For a casual "look-around" I think one may "do" the Republic in about one month.

If you have time for only one section, it is best to determine what, in your opinion, would interest you most. Should you care to see only the châteaux of the Loire Valley, they may be visited in three or four days—even in two, if you omit the less important ones. It is possible to include the Riviera in a journey of one week from Paris back to Paris. The war zone may be covered in one, two, or three days. At least eight or ten days are necessary for a tour of France to include the base of the Pyrenees, Carcassonne, the Gorges of the Tarn, Lourdes, and Pau. This trip might be extended to Biarritz by adding two days.

Should you care to go north from Nice by way of the "Route des Alpes," two days are required to reach Chamonix, where at least two more days should be spent. I am not considering "cures" in my estimates of time. To take a cure usually requires a stay of three weeks in the spa chosen. Sometimes an after-cure is necessary to give a patient time to recuperate from a strenuous treatment. Advice in such matters should come from a physician.

For "Pardons," special fêtes and unusual celebrations, inquiry should be made ahead of time, so that one may plan if possible to be present. Travel agencies usually know in advance when these events are to be celebrated and can give definite information. As they change every year, it is advisable to learn the exact date.

From May to November is the season in France. The weather should be at its best during these months, and most of the important events take place in the spring and summer. Winter is usually anything but pleasant, because of frequent rain, mist, snow, and heavy winds. Some theaters are open during the summer, and there are performances of grand opera, as well as of light opera, in the Opéra Comique when you go to Paris. For an enjoyable tour of France do not attempt anything except the Riviera during the winter. As for expense, you may live in luxury and spend accordingly, or by patronizing hotels which are not "de luxe" and by visiting pensions you may travel comfortably for $7 to $10 a day.

E. M. Newman.

CONTENTS

[ix]

ILLUSTRATIONS

ILLUSTRATIONS

ILLUSTRATIONS

[xiii]

ILLUSTRATIONS

ILLUSTRATIONS

[xv]

ILLUSTRATIONS

[xvi]

ILLUSTRATIONS

[xvii]

ILLUSTRATIONS

I FIRST IMPRESSIONS AT HAVRE

LIKE MELROSE ABBEY IN SCOTLAND, JUMIEGES ABBEY IN NORMANDY
HAUNTS THE MEMORY

SEEING FRANCE

I

FIRST IMPRESSIONS AT HAVRE

NATIONS, like individuals, have certain eccentricities. Call them mannerisms or customs, if you will, but they are distinctive and mark each country as definitely as a boundary line separating one land from another. Were I asked to name the trait that is most characteristically French, I think I should choose thrift as the one that predominates among the masses. To the common people of France, a sou is a sou, and to an even greater extent a franc is a franc.

Unlike the Scot, who is economical because he must be, the Frenchman saves his money because it is his habit to save, as it was of his father before him. In Scotland, the soil in many places is unproductive, and conditions are such as to make life hard; but in La Belle France, nature is bounteous and the peasants, family for family, are among the richest in the world. Why, then, the constant effort to save? Because thrift is inborn with the French peasants. It is not tradition alone; it is almost a religion with them. Gold or silver coins in France often disappear like magic. Where do they go? They go into a sock, a trunk, anywhere to insure secrecy and safety.

Proof of this is found whenever France, in a crisis, calls for funds. Then from hidden nooks come millions, nay billions of francs, a golden hoard, which more than once has saved the country from disaster. If the safety of France were at stake to-day, the peasant would respond instantly with his savings, as he has done under like conditions in the past. His thrift has always been the reservoir from which national emergency funds have been drawn in time of need.

A Frenchman may argue an hour or more over a few sous, or may go into a rage over a single franc, but when his country is in danger he "digs deep." And the same thing is true of the Frenchwoman. I recall an instance. I was taking pictures where a woman had bought the sole right to sell picture-postcards. Tho I carried credentials from the French Government, when the woman discovered me in the act of taking photographs in her town, she rushed at me in a most threatening manner, showering abuse on me and on everyone related to me, and demanding that I cease at once. Explanations were in vain. Shrieking like a madwoman, she ran for help, and several gendarmes rallied promptly to her assistance. The officers demanded that I make off at once.

I was informed that this poor woman had purchased the sole right to sell pictures of that town, and that I was trying to take the bread from her mouth and incidentally to starve her children. It was of no use to explain that I was taking pictures solely for my lectures, that I had no intention of selling any of the views, or that the Government had given me credentials which permitted me to take photos anywhere in France except in the neighborhood of fortifications.

Finally I turned to the infuriated woman and asked what she would charge to permit me to take such photographs as I needed. Bursting with anger, she shouted: "Give me two francs, or you can't take a single picture!" All this fuss for two francs—about ten cents in American money! This may

A LUXURIOUS HOME IN NORMANDY

sound absurd to one who does not know the French peasants, but nothing is more typical of the importance of a franc in the eyes of the average citizen of France.

In recent years many new and up-to-date hotels have risen in various parts of the country, but even now there are towns with hotels that do not contain a single bathroom. To the spoiled American this may seem a great deprivation. I was annoyed when, in a small place in southern France, I asked a landlady where the bathroom was located and was told there was none. In fact, I was politely informed by my indignant hostess that such an inquiry had never before been made; that the people who visited her hotel were clean and did not require a bathroom. If at times the traveler in France is inconvenienced in such a manner, there are other compensations.

[3]

It is rare, even in the smallest town, not to find excellent food, well prepared and made palatable by unusually good cooks. The gourmet will find the cuisine to his liking almost everywhere in France. What he eats may be a matter of taste, but, whatever his preference may be, he will almost always be well satisfied with the preparation of his favorite dish. His stomach may rebel at the thought of eating escargots or snails; he may have no liking for frogs' legs or other dishes peculiarly French, but there is such a variety of appetizing things to eat that one is never at a loss.

Tales have been spread that in some restaurants horseflesh is served. The statement, with reservations, is true; but no butcher may sell horse or mule meat without publicly advertising that fact in front of his shop, and no restaurant except perhaps one in the poorest quarter would serve horse meat without the knowledge of the purchaser. In the better and more fashionable places, horse meat is never sold; so when a visitor goes to a reputable restaurant he may be sure he is eating beef, mutton or lamb, if that is what he orders.

The French criticize us for eating corn on the cob. They regard this as food only for animals. Generally speaking, they do not know what sweet corn is. I have seen them sneer at our Concord or blue-black grapes, and have heard them assert that these taste like ink; if this does not sound well to us, let us be more tactful ourselves when making unkind remarks about snails or frogs' legs. It may be amusing to see the French worker or peasant enter a restaurant and promptly tie a napkin around his neck or tuck it into his collar, as if he were about to be shaved; and afterwards ply a toothpick vigorously in public. Such manners, of course, are not to be found among the French people of refinement, but are confined to the more ignorant classes. We may find places in our own country where the marks of culture are conspicuous by their absence. Taking everything into consideration, no country has perfect manners. The audible sipping of soup is a sound not peculiar to any one country.

I mention these things not because I think them more

AN EIGHT-STORY SKY-SCRAPER IN HAVRE

noticeable in France than elsewhere, but merely to caution the visitor to get away from the habit of forming wrong impressions. Common people are to be found in all countries. In France, more than in other lands, there is a code of politeness that prevails even among servants. One servant always addresses another as Monsieur. "Merci," or "Thank

[5]

you," is invariably offered in return for a service rendered. Politeness is as much a trait among the French as thrift. In this regard the visitor will do well to adopt their ways.

Some Americans who go abroad for the first time object to a continental breakfast, but it is the custom everywhere in continental Europe to serve only coffee and rolls. Fruit, eggs or cereals are extra, even in the best hotels. Europeans are unaccustomed to a heavy breakfast. In France early breakfast is known as "petit déjeuner" or "little breakfast," and is usually served in one's room. Déjeuner or luncheon consists of soup, fish, meat, vegetables, a salad, dessert and coffee. Dinner is the heaviest meal of the day and as a rule includes a number of courses. With the French it is customary to drink wine, both at luncheon and at dinner. No meal, except early breakfast, is considered complete without a glass or

EARLY RISERS AT A POPULAR CHANNEL RESORT

more of wine. In many pensions and hotels it is served as a part of the meal, without extra cost. In first-class restaurants, one is expected to buy wine, altho it is not compulsory. Waiters are naturally disappointed when the cost of a bottle of wine is not added to the check, yet this need not disconcert the traveler. I assume that few Americans go to Europe solely for the benefit of the waiters who serve them.

The French people are less inclined to travel than the people of any other European country. There is nothing in any other land, they say, that cannot be obtained or seen in their own. Their sincerity in this regard will scarcely be questioned by any visitor who has traveled all over France. It is indeed a fair land, and one of wonderful variety. Would you enjoy scenic beauty? It is here in almost every guise, from snow-clad and majestic summits to green and fertile valleys; from deep and narrow gorges, painted by nature in many colors, to mountain lakes, emerald green or bluest of blue; from great cities and wonderful cathedrals to smiling countrysides and vineyards dotted with quiet villages.

Do you seek art? The galleries of France are filled with the choicest collections of the world's masterpieces; some of the finest examples of Greek sculpture are to be found in the French treasure-houses of art. Are you interested in architecture? France has buildings representing every period, from Grecian, Roman, Rococo, Renaissance, down to modern times. Here are the finest Gothic cathedrals in the world. Amphitheaters, bridges, churches, whatever you may prefer, all are to be seen in this great country.

There are no more magnificent resorts than those which line the seashore and crown the heights of France. Do you enjoy society? Are you intrigued by the smart set? If so, you may look upon some of the most beautiful creations of

BRINGING IN THE LIFE-BOAT FOR THE NIGHT

the designers of Paris, worn at various resorts by women famous in the world of fashion. Would chance tempt you? Here are race-tracks where many thousands gather to see pedigreed horses run, and incidentally to wager large sums on their favorite animals. And there are the numerous casinos where men take a fling at roulette, chemin-de-fer, and other games devoted to the siren, fickle fortune.

"This," say the people of France, "is why we have no need to travel. There is nothing which any other country offers, that we cannot have at home." It is another trait for which the French are known. Pride of country, nationalism—patriotism, if you prefer—is always evident among them.

There are many ways of arriving in France, many stations on the border that separates it from other European states.

The majority of American visitors arrive by steamer, and from a watery gateway obtain the first glimpse of the beautiful country in which they are about to spend days, weeks or months. And of these portals there are many. Certain steamers deposit their passengers at Cherbourg, while others go to Havre, Brest, or the Mediterranean ports. Even in the crossing from England, there are several routes from which a choice may be made, depending very largely upon one's immediate destination in France and the saving of time in reaching it. For visitors who go direct from London to Paris, the air route has become popular; but those who prefer trains and boats are likely to select the short Channel crossing between Dover and Calais. The ribbon of water that divides the two countries—it is easy to see from shore to shore on a clear day—is likely to be boisterous, and altho the steamship companies try to make the passage as comfortable as possible, passengers are unlikely to find pleasure in it and are glad to make it brief. Other popular routes for the crossing are from Folkestone to Boulogne, and from Newhaven to Dieppe. The one from Southampton to Havre or Cherbourg also is sometimes convenient.

Let us assume that we have arrived at Havre. Altho the majority of American travelers pass from the gangway of the ship to a waiting train that carries them swiftly to Paris, we shall pursue a more

A FRENCH LIFE-GUARD

HAVRE, NEXT TO MARSEILLES, IS THE MOST IMPORTANT SEAPORT IN FRANCE

leisurely course, and gain an impression of the whole country and its people, customs, art, architecture, recreations, labor, transportation, agriculture, food, and endeavor to arrive at a proper appreciation of the soul of France, instead of forming our estimate and conclusions after a glance around Paris alone.

Havre itself is unlikely to detain us long, because it is not a city of sights, altho it has had a notable history and to-day is a busy commercial city and naval base. It serves the purpose of giving the visitor a foretaste of later experiences. First of all, he realizes that he has arrived in a distinctly foreign country, which is not so apparent after arrival in England, where the people speak a familiar language. And language here is not all that produces the thrill of novelty. The people are different from those in the tourist's own country. They dress differently, and immediately one observes a difference also in their manner of transacting such small affairs as the stamping of passports, the examination of luggage, the conveying of one to the hotel, the service at the hotel, the furnishings, the food and its preparation, shopping —all is foreign and different from the American methods and customs. Thus the traveler finds delight at every turn in observing how the rest of the world lives—especially if he is not too certain that the American way is the only way.

Havre was founded in the sixteenth century, and under Napoleon it was raised to the rank of a first-class naval harbor. Much of its present importance is due to its transatlantic passenger service and its trade in cotton and coffee. The most interesting excursion in the city is around the docks, which occupy a vast water frontage. The main thoroughfare is the Rue de Paris, which brings us to the Musée. This contains a good provincial art collection that includes

HAVRE CULTIVATES BEAUTY, EVEN AROUND ITS CITY HALL

paintings by such moderns as Millet, Pissarro, Forain, and Monet. The Church of Notre Dame has an unattractive exterior, and the interior is not of interest. Northwest of the city is a distant suburb, Ste. Adresse, which was the seat of the Belgian government after the fall of Antwerp in the Great War. It is said to have obtained its name from the legend that on a ship driven to the foot of the Cap de la Heve, the sailors declined to obey the commands of the captain and invoked St. Denis to save them. The captain remonstrated: "You should ask help not from St. Denis but from Sainte Adresse, for Adresse [skill] alone can bring us to port." After that, the sailors worked with a will, and after reaching Cap de la Heve they gave the place the name of the saint.

There are several good restaurants in Havre outside of the hotels, so we enjoy our first French dinner on French soil and (forgetting that the menu and style of cooking vary in different parts of the country) arrive at the conclusion that we are to derive much pleasure from the cuisine that is said to be the best in the world. It cannot be denied that France has sent her chefs to all parts of the earth, proclaiming the superiority of French cookery and influencing the dinners of the world. Around Havre, it may be a surprize to visitors to observe that cider is a popular beverage, and that in many of the smaller establishments, at least, the usual *vin ordinaire* does not appear upon the table unless it is ordered; but we have arrived in a country where wine with meals seems just about as indispensable as knives, forks, and table napery.

We are likely to be impressed by the variety of food offered, and by the many courses that are considered necessary to constitute a meal. An American of my acquaintance observed that the chief ingredients of the French cuisine must be garlic and olive oil. This was an exaggeration, of course, and was more applicable to the food served in the South, particularly in the Marseilles district, than to what reaches the tables of the North; but it is true that the Frenchman enjoys his meats served with highly flavored sauces, his salads bearing the unmistakable flavor (and odor) of garlic and tarragon, and his soups steaming the pungent essences of garden herbs. All are attractively served, carefully selected and prepared, and the novice soon comes to enjoy them, especially if he has been eating the comparatively flavorless food of England or even the more "natural" American dishes.

As we take our inevitable soup, followed by chicken *chasseur* (chicken is always present in France, as are mutton and roast beef in England), ragout of mutton, rabbit *garenne*, and one of the vast variety of omelets, with salad, tarts, cheese, fruit and coffee, we are likely to recall what Gustave

HOW LE HAVRE HONORS HER SONS WHO FELL IN THE WORLD WAR

Flaubert wrote about a table spread for a wedding "break-fast." Sometimes we hear that the French are not meat-eaters, tho it is possible that the meat habit has increased in modern times; at any rate, a vegetarian diet does not appeal to the natives of Normandy. Flaubert, who was born at Rouen, said the table had upon it "four joints of beef, six fricasseed chickens, stewed veal, three legs of mutton, and in the middle was a whole suckling pig. At the corners were placed brandy in carafes and sweet cider in bottles, and all the glasses on the board were already filled to their limits. There were great dishes of yellow cream, which shook at the least shock given the table, . . . cakes and tarts."

The inhabitants of Havre take great pride in their Rue de Paris, and particularly in the café-bordered Place Gambetta, where one may hear many languages and observe sailors of many complexions enjoying themselves—yellow or black boys from Martinique and Guadeloupe, Greeks, Lascars, Chinese, Portuguese, English, and occasionally Americans. One who desires a glimpse of this side of life has the chance here to witness a vivid picture; altho the stranger is advised not to wander around the wharf-side during the night hours, for some of these strangers in port bring their own customs with them, and they do not always coincide with what is recognized as western behavior.

One who speaks French fluently may find difficulty with the patois that is commonly spoken in this part of France. To understand the language of a country in which one is traveling is always a convenience, of course; yet almost any-where in France the English language suffices for the tourist. At the hotels, restaurants, and other places likely to attract the visitor, someone seems always at hand to act as inter-preter. Victor Hugo wrote: "Oh, you brave Normans!

Know you that your patois is venerable and sacred. It is a flower which sprang from the same root as the French. Your patois has left its impress upon the speech of England, Sicily, and Judea, at London, Naples, and the tomb of Christ. To lose your speech is to lose your nationality, therefore in preserving your idiom you are preserving your patriotism."

There are many pleasant rambles in the immediate vicinity of the city, and in the course of them one is reminded that Havre was the birthplace of many men and women whose reputations extended around the world; for example, of Madeleine de Scudéry, the seventeenth-century author of voluminous romances; of Bernardin de Saint-Pierre, author of "Paul et Virginie"; and of the poet, Casimir Delavigne. Around the mouth of the Seine, we also recall that Canada was discovered by men of Havre, Dieppe and Honfleur, who

HAVRE IS JUSTLY PROUD OF ITS PUBLIC GARDENS

TREASURE SEEKERS ON THE CHANNEL SANDS

accompanied Champlain and whose descendants retain the speech of their forefathers in the new land. There are many people hereabouts who still think of North America as "La Normandie Transatlantique."

A popular excursion from the city is to the lighthouses on the cliffs. Another is to Graville, about two miles eastward, thence upward to the eleventh-century church of the ancient Abbey of Ste. Honorine. At the left of the altar is the despoiled tomb of the saint—a sarcophagus open at the end, through which it was possible to view the sacred relics. They were· removed at the time of the Norman invasion; but pilgrimages to the Abbey of Graville continued for a long time afterwards. There is a splendid view of the harbor and of Havre from the wooded graveyard, particularly at night, when the lights from the boats and city streets seem like

[17]

glow-worms in the valley below. At such a time one can see beauty in this busy port.

From Graville we may go to Harfleur, or we may make the journey of less than four miles direct from Havre. Harfleur has a notable history, but it attracts slight attention to-day, save from travelers on their way to Château d'Orcher, which has fine shaded avenues that command a pretty view of the Seine. There are artists who consider this view the finest in Normandy.

From Havre, being leisurely travelers, we can go to Rouen by steamer; and the views along the river well repay us for the day's journey. Tickets purchased at the agencies usually make it optional with the passenger—river or railroad—and it is likely that the great majority of excursionists patronize the iron horse. After covering some of this river territory,

THE QUAINT OLD HARBOR OF HONFLEUR, NEAR HAVRE

as long ago as 1689, Madame de Sévigné wrote: "I have seen the most beautiful country in all the world; I have seen all the charms of the beautiful Seine and the most agreeable prairies in the world." The modern traveler, who has seen other great rivers and "prairies," may not use so many superlatives in regard to the banks of the lower Seine; but he cannot fail to be similarly enthusiastic concerning the voyage between the sea and Rouen, which nearly two thousand years ago was the capital of a Roman province, and is to-day a thriving and important modern city.

The Seine has been called "the main street of that elongated metropolis which extends from the Ile de la Cité in Paris to Havre." The French like to think of it that way. Michelet refers to it as "the most civilized and the most perfect of the rivers of France," and adds that "it bears the spirit of Paris to Normandy, to the sea, to England, and to far-away America." When he was first consul, Napoleon predicted that the time would come when Havre, Rouen and Paris would be one and the same city and the Seine its grand highway. One with vision may feel that this prophecy has been fulfilled—at least figuratively—because the banks of the river are lined with villages and settlements that give the appearance of a continuous city.

The shifting sands at the mouth of the river are avoided by the Tancarville Canal, which runs from Havre to Harfleur and to Tancarville, where it joins the river. Above Harfleur we see the towers of the Château de Tancarville, which dates from the eleventh century and once was the home of the seigneurs. A triangular fortress-castle it is, having at each angle a great tower, and occupying an imposing position. Rare privileges were granted to its occupants by William the Conqueror, and the place was of great impor-

"HELLO!"

tance to the Dukes of Normandy and to their successors, the Kings of France. The castle's frowning walls prompt recollection of several of its famous inmates: Agnes Sorel; Mary Queen of Scots, who spent a part of her childhood here; John Law, creator of the disastrous Mississippi Bubble; and the Duchesse de Nemours, author of famous memoirs.

There is a beautiful drive overland from Tancarville to Lillebonne, which we reach by water. This pretty town is about midway between Havre and Rouen, and is one of the oldest in France. It is thought that Julius Cæsar or Augustus built a Roman city upon the ruins of the capital city of the Caletas, and named it Julia Bona, in honor of a farmer's daughter, which accounts for the modern name. The Roman amphitheater is the most northerly in Europe, and it remains to-day the strongest evidence of the ancient importance of the town. Doubtless it dates from the second century and was capable of holding three thousand spectators. Excavations have been in progress here for over a century, and there has been a good harvest of antiquities, many of which repose in the museum at Rouen. Several of the ranges of stone seats were utilized in the construction of the famous Abbey of St. Wandrille. Among the important mosaics uncovered was a hunting scene supposed to represent Diana or Apollo; and it seems likely that there are others still awaiting the picks and shovels of archeologists. Parts of the ruined castle of William the Conqueror remain, and the town has an interesting medieval church dating from the fourteenth century.

We arrive at Caudebec-en-Caux, a picturesque old town that well repays a visit. The artist Vernet is said to have considered the view from the quay the finest in France; others have been similarly enthusiastic, one at least having declared that the town itself was located here for the purpose of making the view more beautiful. It is here that the *mascaret* or spring tidal bore rolls up the river—a rushing wave or series of waves often fourteen or fifteen feet high, similar to that at Hangchow, China, and several other places. It is vastly interesting to the crowds that gather to see it, but disastrous to any small shipping that may be unprepared for its approach. A witness of the phenomenon has written: "The river was smooth as glass till suddenly just below Ville-

A QUIET NOOK IN CAUDEBEC

CAUDEBEC HAS AN OLD CATHEDRAL WITH A BEAUTIFUL TOWER

quier there appeared first a speck of foam in the midst of the stream, and then the water seemed to rise in its whole width and to roll majestically up to Caudebec, the sides of the wave dashing stones and spray far inshore on either side; the whole mass of water came on roaring and thundering in a wave about six feet high, and swept on as far as we could see; two or three waves followed, and these broke furiously over the quay. For about ten minutes the broad calm river was like a stormy sea of raging foam, wave dashing against wave in struggling fury, and then, almost at once, the tumult disappeared." The daughter of Victor Hugo and her husband and child were drowned at Villequier, where they are buried.

We are unlikely to be at Caudebec at the hour of the *mascaret,* but we shall find much there to interest us; for example, the market-place with its hotels, where one may dine on the balcony and watch the animated land and river scenes below. Then there are the splendid old timbered buildings, some of them dating from the thirteenth century, and the Church of Notre Dame, in flamboyant Gothic style—a church often considered one of the best in the see of Rouen. The square tower has an octagonal spire, which rises in three stages, like the papal crown. There is a fine triple porch and a balustrade surrounding the church, in which are carved letters three feet high, spelling words of the Magnificat and "Salve Regina." The interior of the edifice contains fifteenth and sixteenth century stained glass and several interesting architectural features. Henry IV is credited with having called it the most beautiful church he had ever seen.

There is a delightful walk along the Seine to St. Gertrude, which has an unusual church with a stone tabernacle above the altar. Even more enticing to the tourist is the walk of

[23]

less than three miles to the celebrated and ancient Abbey of St. Wandrille, founded in the seventh century. The building suffered from invaders, and in the seventeenth century the spire crashed to earth and destroyed much of the existing structure. The cloister remains, however, and the convent buildings have been converted into a modern residence, at one time occupied by the symbolist poet, Maurice Maeterlinck. With Georgette Leblanc, the actress, Maeterlinck directed Shakespearean performances here for an audience of guests, who followed the performers from place to place in each change of scene, all of which was reported in the American magazines and newspapers at the time.

The founder of the Abbey was St. Wandrille, a disciple of St. Columba, and it became a famous seat of learning with over three hundred resident monks. The Abbey sent out

EVEN THE HOTELS OF CAUDEBEC HAVE A TOUCH OF QUAINTNESS

evangelists, who had much to do with the conversion of the whole province. More than forty persons once resident here have been canonized, among them Saints Agathon, Ansbart, and Lambert. There is record of a holy font here, now gone, upon which was engraved: "He who takes the holy water without having immersed the hand, does a thing dishonest, and must ask pardon of God."

WHERE NATURE IS GRADUALLY WINNING A LONG
FIGHT WITH MAN

Another pleasant excursion from Caudebec is to Ville-quier, which lies less than three miles away. We pass en route a chapel dating from the thirteenth century. It is a tradition at Caudebec that the newly married should visit this chapel on their wedding day. A château of the time of Louis XV commands a fine view of the river, and it is said that the *mascaret* may best be observed from this point.

[25]

We pass the market-town of Duclair and arrive at the Abbey of Jumièges, said to be the most ancient monastery in Normandy, as it was founded by St. Philibert in the seventh century. It was powerful, celebrated and rich; some of its abbots were beatified and others were made archbishops. When in the neighborhood, it was the privilege and custom of the Dukes of Normandy and the Kings of England and France to lodge beneath its roof. The founder received permission from Clovis and his Queen to build the abbey upon the site of an ancient fortress, and within ten years it was occupied by eight hundred monks. Invaders pillaged the institution, tortured the monks until they revealed hidden treasures, and finally fire completed the ruin. Only two monks remained. After the second Duke of Normandy escaped death while hunting, however, in the tenth century,

INSIDE THE ANCIENT ABBEY AT JUMIEGES

he gave orders to have the abbey rebuilt. William the Conqueror reserved the Isle of Helling in Norfolk for the benefit of the monks. The abbey had several other powerful protectors, but it declined after the Calvinist Reformation.

There is a legend that in 658 the founder of Jumièges learned that a boat had run aground in the river, and that in it were two youths, whose arms and legs were bleeding from cruel mutilation. He received them, and the monks

TOWERS A THOUSAND YEARS OLD
Front view of Jumièges Abbey

tended them with great care, so that they recovered and took the vows of the order. Clovis and his Queen visited the monastery and Philibert learned that the two youths were the sons of the King. They had rebelled against their father, who was making a pilgrimage to the Holy Land, and their mother had decreed that they should be deprived of their bodily strength. Their majesties were delighted to see their sons again, however, and in gratitude bestowed rich gifts and privileges upon the abbey. There are several ruins of great historic and artistic interest in the vicinity, and anyone who has the leisure should not fail to visit them. Charles VII and Agnes Sorel, his mistress, frequently lodged at Jumièges, and it was here that she died—perhaps of poison. She bequeathed her heart to the monks of the abbey. The relic was placed beneath a stone still to be seen at the museum, which also contains the tomb of Nicolas Lerous, one of the judges of Jeanne d'Arc.

There is still another notable ecclesiastical monument that claims our attention before we arrive at Rouen, and that is St. Georges de Boscherville, one of the most perfect specimens of Norman architecture in France. It has been more fortunate than some of the others, and altho it was founded in the eleventh century, its abbey church is to-day considered an architectural marvel. It is a magnificent edifice that easily could accommodate five thousand people.

The Seine makes a triple bend as we approach Rouen, and we pass beside splendid forests, in which are set pretty industrial villages and the villas of rich manufacturers of the Norman metropolis. It will be more convenient for us to visit Le Petit Couronne by ferry, after we have arrived at Rouen; but as we see it on this river tour, let us promise ourselves to visit the village for one reason, and not pass it by, as do most Americans; for it contains the home of Pierre Corneille, and has become a literary shrine of vast interest. It was purchased by the Department of the Lower Seine and has become a museum devoted to the great poet. There are here many relics of him and many works of art belonging to his time.

At the beginning of the voyage up the Seine from Havre to Rouen, we assumed that we had disembarked at the former port from our transatlantic steamer and were making a leisurely journey toward Paris. In the same way, let us assume that on another occasion we have arrived in France at Cherbourg, where so many of the Atlantic liners discharge their passengers for the European journey. As at Liverpool, Southampton, and Havre, the visitor is anxious to arrive at the capital, so there is usually time for no more than a glance at Cherbourg as the steamer train pulls away from the wharf-side to make a quick run to Paris.

The city deserves more than that from the visitor, how-ever; it is the most convenient portal to many places in west-ern Normandy that should not be overlooked. Cherbourg is on the site of the ancient Gallic port of Coriallo, in all probability, altho there are writers who declare that it was founded by Julius Cæsar or one of his lieutenants; doubtless this conclusion is based on the fact that during the Middle Ages the place was known as Cæsariburgus. Its ancient castle, which was said to be the strongest in the world, has disappeared; but beneath the modern streets there have been found subterranean passages that may have had connection with the stronghold. Cherbourg is protected by a famous breakwater that was commenced in the eighteenth century by Louis XVI, and the first Napoleon took a lively interest in the building of a foundation for a battery of twenty guns. Altho violent seas have wrecked this at various times, repairs have been made and the fortifications of the city are notable for their size and strength.

The Hôtel de Ville houses a museum that contains several worth-while paintings: Van Dyck's "Meleager and Atalanta," an inn scene by Teniers, Poussin's "Pyramus and Thisbe," Murillo's "Christ Bearing the Cross," Jordaens's "Adoration of the Magi," and Fra Angelico's "Entombment."

In the Place Napoléon is a bronze equestrian statue of the Emperor, on the pedestal of which are engraved his words: "I had resolved to renew at Cherbourg the wonders of Egypt."

Several delightful excursions may be made from Cher-bourg. Only five miles away is Martinvast, with a sixteenth-century castle. At Tourlaville, less than three miles distant, is a good example of a feudal castle. Five miles away is Querqueville, with an interesting seventeenth-century church. On the peninsula near the city is the parish of Greville, the birthplace of the painter, Jean François Millet, the house being marked by a tablet. It is a pleasant artistic pilgrimage to this home of the creator of "The Angelus," one of the best-known pictures in the world. Millet waged a long battle against poverty. He said: "They wish to force me into their drawing-room art to break my spirit. But no, no; I was born a peasant and a peasant I will die. I will say what I feel." Not far away is the De Tocqueville château, and within a radius of ten or fifteen miles there are several places that are likely to prove of interest during several days of sightseeing. Cherbourg now has good hotels, and it is no hardship to remain there for a week. Things have changed greatly since the Englishman wrote: "Cherbourg is not a place for residence longer than is necessary. I was obliged to go to a vile hole, little better than a hog-sty, where for a miserable, dirty, wretched chamber, two suppers composed chiefly of a plate of apples and some butter and cheese, with some trifle besides, too bad to eat, and one miserable dinner, they brought me a bill of nearly thirty shillings." The lodgings are comfortable nowadays, and nobody complains about the quality or the quantity of the food.

11 INLAND FROM CHERBOURG

MONT SAINT-MICHEL AT HIGH TIDE, SEEN FROM THE CAUSEWAY

II

INLAND FROM CHERBOURG

THERE are many towns and cities not far from the coast that offer much of novelty and interest to one who visits them for the first time; and each contributes to one's appreciation and knowledge of Normandy.

First of all, let us go to Valognes, a clean, well built town which, with its four thousand inhabitants, holds but a modest position in the world to-day. Perhaps there is slight evidence of its great past, as one takes a rapid glance at its exterior; and yet it is claimed that, previous to the Revolution, Valognes was the residence of "one hundred families of distinguished birth and fortune, and since that period it has been the home of many of the old noblesse." Long before the time of the aristocrats, however, it was an important Roman town called Alauna; and in later centuries it loomed in the destinies of William the Conqueror, Edward III, and Henry III. The castle was ordered destroyed by Louis XIV, and few of the great ecclesiastical monuments have endured until the present time. Once it was a center of the glove and cloth industries, but now it is known chiefly as the center of an agricultural district.

Valognes is a charming old town, and one will find pleasure in taking a seat in the Place du Château and observing the somewhat sedate and quiet life of the community. In the old theater is the library and a good collection of ancient sarcophagi and other antiquities. The church of Notre Dame is

[33]

said to possess the only Gothic dome in France. It is a peculiar edifice, with steeple, tower and dome almost touching one another. Inside we find several good examples of carving and glass.

From here we ramble on to the suburb of Alleaume, pass ancient ruins that are popularly known as the Vieux Château, and about one-half mile farther to the remains of the Roman town, with remnants of the amphitheater and baths, said to have been destroyed in the third century. Medals and coins have been found here in recent years, which prompts a recollection of the old saw that the ancient Romans, particularly the soldiers, must have had pockets with holes in them, for wherever they are known to have been, one is likely to come upon the tell-tale evidence in coins—even beneath bridges which they are known to have crossed frequently. Alleaume

A VIEW IN NORMANDY ALONG THE ENGLISH CHANNEL

has a fourteenth-century church in which there is a famous statue of the Virgin.

There are numerous pleasant walks and drives around Valognes. About seven miles away is the Trappist monastery of Notre Dame de Grace de la Trappe, noted for its cheese-making. The inmates are bound to eternal silence by their vows, and there is what most people would con-

UNDER FULL SAIL OFF THE NORMANDY COAST

sider a too-rigid discipline in regard to food and hours of sleep. They adhere to the belief that "sins must be expiated either by penitence in this life or by fire in the next."

The town of Carentan is famous for its butter, which certain connoisseurs have declared to be the best in France. The town has the air of prosperity, due to its milk industry. There are several old arcaded houses that are picturesque, and the rebuilt church has several good features. The western entrance has an example of what is known as "dog-tooth" ornamentation; the central tower has an open-work steeple, and there are many figures and gargoyles upon the exterior. A canal connects the town with the sea, and it is pleasant to stroll in the shade of the elm groves along its banks.

One of the splendid small towns of France is Bayeux, which deserves a visit for several reasons, notably its Cathedral and the celebrated Tapestry. The place has only seven thousand inhabitants, but it has a much more important history than many of the large cities. On account of its chief church and collection of old houses, it has been compared to

Chester, England, and there is considerable resemblance between the two. Our first excursion is likely to be to the Cathedral. The bishopric of Bayeux was founded in the fourth century, and among the ecclesiastics who have held the high office are several men who loom large in French history; for example, Odo, half-brother of William the Conqueror, who held the office for fifty years. It is possible that only the crypt remains of Odo's church; but it is of ancient

A NORMAN IDEA OF LAWN DECORATION

construction throughout and in an excellent state of preservation. The crypt, supported by pillars with curious capitals, and having traces of wall paintings, dates at least from the eleventh century. The chapter house has thirteenth-century floor tiles and frescoes, and the treasury has several rare objects, among them an ivory chest having applied silverwork and an ancient stole and chasuble, said to have belonged to St. Regnobert.

South of the Cathedral is the Old Bishop's Palace, in which

is a library of thirty thousand volumes. This will not detain us, however, and we pass along to the celebrated Bayeux Tapestry, which Napoleon caused to be exhibited in various parts of France when desiring to gain support for his proposed invasion of England. The embroidery, which is twenty inches wide, is seventy-seven yards long and is said to have been presented to Odo in the seventh century, altho there is

ON THE ROOF: A CAT-FIGHT THAT NEVER ENDS

no certainty as to its early history. It has fifty-eight scenes, each accompanied by a Latin inscription. Wace, a canon of Bayeux, was the author of the "Roman de Rou," which he dedicated to Henry II, and the Tapestry illustrates its scenes. It was barely known to the world before the middle of the eighteenth century; but it has been considered a priceless work of art since that time. The scenes range from the promise of Edward the Confessor to bequeath his throne to William to the death of Harold at Hastings.

There are several other interesting sights in Bayeux, and the traveler may spend a profitable day here; but he is likely to be on his way after he has remained a few hours. The old town is the home of the State Tapestry Factory, which was founded only two years after the famous Gobelins. The Palace of Justice was two hundred years old when in a near-by factory the manufacture of Beauvais tapestry began. It is intended chiefly for furniture. Landscapes, flowers, animals, and pastoral scenes constitute the principal designs. The beauty and brightness of the colors, the delicacy of the shading and the durability of the material have made it renowned.

The road from Bayeux to St. Lô offers much to the visitor. For example, he will be pleased by the various fine examples of what have been called "fortified farms." These are common throughout Normandy—farms surrounded by high walls and towers, which give them the appearance of fortifications when viewed from a distance. St. Lô is upon a hill, the situation probably having been for defense, which was required in the Middle Ages. The Abbey of St. Croix was founded here by Charlemagne and the riverside was strongly fortified. The town and castle near by received the name of St. Lô from St. Laudus, who was an early bishop of the district.

Let us go to the pleasantly named Place des Beaux Regards, which is in front of the magnificent Church of Notre Dame. Originally this was a collegiate church, and it has towers more imposing than any others in Normandy. Here we observe a fifteenth-century open-air stone pulpit, which is unusual in a French church. In the square is a statue of a pretty water-carrier, and if we look carefully we may see

STATUE OF WILLIAM THE CONQUEROR AT FALAISE

CASTLE OF WILLIAM THE CONQUEROR AT FALAISE

VIEW OF FALAISE FROM THE CASTLE OF WILLIAM THE CONQUEROR

the village maidens carrying jars and assuming the exact pose of the statue.

A short journey brings us to Coutances, the ancient city of Cosedia and Constantia. It nestles around its beautiful Cathedral, which sits upon a hill fully three hundred feet above the surrounding plain. Here, in a town of about seven thousand inhabitants, is one of the prettiest public gardens in northern France. From the garden we obtain a view of the famous aqueduct, its five remaining arches overgrown with ivy. Originally there were sixteen of them, as proved by the foundations. The aqueduct is said to occupy the site of an ancient Roman structure, the theory springing from the fact that many Roman coins have been found beneath it. The great glory of Coutances, however, is its Cathedral, the present edifice probably dating from the thirteenth century.

Its spires rise to a height of two hundred fifty feet, and the lantern, called Le Plomb, to one hundred eighty-six feet. "Who was the sublime madman," wrote Vauban, "who dared launch such a monument in the air?" There is a splendid landscape visible from Le Plomb—the promontory of Granville, the coastland of Brittany, and St. Malo far across the bay. The windows, some of them dating from the fourteenth century, show scenes from the lives of St. Lô and St. Marcouf.

Another church that deserves a visit here is St. Pierre, the central tower of which has been termed "an architectural joke and a very quaint and delightful one." Here we find much of architectural interest and some painted glass of the sixteenth century.

Near by is Granville, with its picturesque harbor. The

A LOVELY NORMAN GARDEN AT AVRANCHES

[41]

MONT ST. MICHEL'S MAIN STREET

town is situated at the head of a promontory, and it has recently become a summer resort of the first rank, with palatial hotels. It now has about twelve thousand inhabitants, and while it is considered fashionable, there is much about it that smacks of the simple life of the sturdy sailors who make up a majority of its inhabitants. Granville is only seven miles from the Iles Chausey, of which there are about three hundred. At Granville there is an extreme difference between high and low tide, amounting to about forty-six feet.

Many of the Norman lawns are adorned with porcelain imitations of animals and birds. It is a common sight to come upon a dog apparently tied to a kennel or ready to pounce on a trespasser. This has the advantage of serving the purpose of a real dog without the expense of having to feed the animal. One may have cats meowing on his roof, rabbits running over the lawn, birds in the trees, and chickens in the barnyard. If one has a pond, he may fill it with ducks and geese or add a few frogs to complete the picture. Farmhouses crowd closely upon each other as we motor over the highways. The population is dense. Villages are never more than a few miles apart and practically all the land is under cultivation. In some of the old manors are huge fireplaces with kettles suspended over logs. In all Norman towns river laundries are a feature. Along every stream are covered sheds where women come daily with their household linen. These open-air laundries are as familiar in France as windmills in Holland.

In the little town of Falaise, William the Conqueror was born in 1027. Picturesquely situated in a valley, the ruined Castle of William rises majestically above it. The bronze equestrian statue of the Conqueror is conspicuously placed in a central square. Around its base are statues of the first six Dukes of Normandy. The castle where William was born is a picturesque ruin dating back to the tenth century. It is finely situated on a rugged promontory jutting out over the valley. It was from one of the windows in this castle that Robert the Devil first saw Arlette, the tanner's daughter, whom he later married. She became the mother of William.

MUSEUM ON THE ROCK OF MONT ST. MICHEL

THE "GREAT DEGREE" LEADING
UP TO THE ABBEY

Avranches would not have as many visitors as it has, were it not for its lovely garden and the magnificent view of the Bay of St. Michel. We walk through it to a terrace which overlooks the bay.

Like a pyramid rising from the sea is picturesque Mont St. Michel. From this distance only its pyramidal shape holds our attention; it seems too small to be of much importance, yet the rock is one hundred sixty feet in height. Until 1880 it was isolated at high tide; since that time a dike has connected it with the mainland, so that one may reach the island at high or low tide by motoring over a causeway. When the tide is out, hundreds of cars are parked on the beach, but luckless indeed is the owner of a car if he does not heed the incoming tide. With the speed of a race-horse the waters of the sea sweep inland, covering miles of bare mudflats in an incredibly short time. The one street of the village is lined with curio shops and restaurants, where lobsters, alive or boiled, are dangled temptingly before the eyes of the visitor.

A long flight of stone steps leads to the Abbey above. After a laborious climb, we arrive at the Great Degree, which means that there is just one more long ascent before we arrive at the entrance to the Abbey. When Louis XI founded the order of the Knighthood of Saint-Michel, in the fifteenth century, the former banquet hall was made the Knights'

GREAT HALL IN THE ABBEY THAT CROWNS MONT ST. MICHEL

ABBEY CLOISTER, A MASTERPIECE OF THE THIRTEENTH CENTURY

Hall. This superb room has three rows of gigantic columns, and at one end is an open fireplace where logs were burned. Adjoining the Abbey is the famous cloister with two hundred columns of polished granite. Exquisite carving embellishes the pointed arches supported by twin columns. The museum contains many interesting relics. One of these is the treadmill within which prisoners of an earlier day plodded wearily to keep the great wheel revolving. All the supplies for the Mount were hoisted up an inclined plane by means of ropes attached to the treadmill. If one is interested in the history of the island and its remarkable church, a brief visit to the museum is worth while. Perched on the top of this high rock, its situation is unique.

One may make the journey around the island when the tide is out. It is hardly possible to accomplish the walk dry-

IN THE ABBEY CHURCH OF MONT ST. MICHEL

shod, as the outgoing tide
leaves a sea of mud behind it.
On the way round the rock,
one may visit a small chapel.
Fisher-folk follow the outgoing waters and pick up
many crabs, shrimps, and
lobsters. Each receding tide
leaves behind a harvest of
crustaceans, for which there
is a ready demand among the
thousands of visitors. Built
originally as a fortification
and later crowned by an Abbey for the Benedictine fa-
thers, Mont St. Michel is to-
day one of the architectural

TREADMILL WHEEL ONCE USED TO
HOIST PROVISIONS AT MONT ST.
MICHEL

curiosities of Europe. There are few places in France that
attract more visitors.

Best known of the many restaurants and hotels on the
island is the establishment founded by Madame Poulard,
famous for its omelets. Visitors who do not care to stop
overnight usually go to this restaurant if for no other reason
than to tell their friends that they indulged in one of these
renowned omelets, which are good but expensive.

Time should determine whether or not one shall remain
overnight on Mont St. Michel, but I would recommend it
if one can spare an extra day. It is worth while just to see
the tide come racing in from the ocean. The view at night
from the causeway, after the island and its houses, piled one
above another, are lighted, also is a sufficient reason for stop-
ping over.

[47]

ON THE SANDS OUTSIDE OF ST. MALO'S ANCIENT WALLS

Founded by the Welsh monk St. Malo, the walled city of that name is now one of the favorite Norman resorts. St. Malo has been besieged many times; one of the most determined onslaughts was made by the Duke of Marlborough in 1758. To-day the British enter its gates, but come as peaceful visitors, crowding the hotels within its walls. St. Malo, with its unpretentious hotels, appeals to the British, who prefer the simplicity of this resort to some of the more fashionable places along the Norman coast. It is a short and inexpensive journey from England to France, and a holiday at St. Malo is a popular diversion. British visitors live here more cheaply than in their own resorts. St. Malo has its casino where during the season the guests are entertained by concerts or opera. Those who are so inclined may play roulette or baccarat, or dance to American jazz music. As in most French resorts, every form of amusement is provided.

III NORTHERN COAST RESORTS

TROUVILLE, THE CONEY ISLAND OF FRANCE

III

NORTHERN COAST RESORTS

LET us assume that we have crossed from England to Dieppe, which is a port city of importance, but has also become a fashionable watering-place. The general outlook is reminiscent of what we have just left on the other side of the Channel, chiefly the white cliffs; but ashore, one quickly realizes that he is not in an English resort. There is a promenade, where French fashionables display their finery; the hotels are expensive, the casino attracts a crowd, and there is a fine beach where mixed bathing is permitted. A French atmosphere is apparent to all newcomers, and Dieppe is a merry place for extended holidays in the late summer.

Dieppe was colonized by Norse adventurers in the tenth century, and to them it owes its name, which derives from the depth of its harbor. It was the home of adventurous corsairs, who made bold voyages and attacks upon cities in England, Portugal, and even the Gold Coast. The earliest castle here was built by Henry II of England, and under Francis I it was even more populous than it is in our time. Its carved ivory became famous in this period, and to-day in the Grande Rue we observe many shops which offer ivory-ware as their specialty. The town has been ruthlessly bombarded, and perhaps its modern appearance is chiefly due to the destruction inflicted on it by the English fleet in 1694, which caused it to be completely rebuilt.

There is an animated scene daily in the fish-market, when the trawlers return and dispose of their catch. This is a never-failing source of interest to tourists. The general market is also a magnet for visitors on market days, when the crowds of hard-featured countrywomen are offering their produce for sale, mostly vegetables and poultry. And this market is in the shadow of the picturesque Church of St. Jacques, certain to attract one's attention during his first ramble about the streets of Dieppe. St. Jacques was begun in the thirteenth century, but it took three hundred years to complete it. Approached from the east, it shows richly decorated flying buttresses; above the west entrance is a square tower, which may be mounted in two hundred and thirty-two steps. Two of the chief features of the interior are the richly carved stone screen and the elaborate roofing of the

AN ENGLISH STEAMER AT THE WHARF IN DIEPPE

WATER FRONT OF DIEPPE SEEN FROM THE CLIFF

Lady Chapel. In the sacristy is a tablet to the memory of Jean d'Ango, usually described as corsair and merchant prince, and quite likely the most celebrated citizen of Dieppe. He was a ship-owner, gained a great fortune from the Indies, and entertained Francis I in elaborate style, for which he received the title of Viscount and Commandant of the Castle and Town of Dieppe.

From the harbor we ascend to the Castle, which dates only from the fifteenth century. From here we obtain an excellent view of the town and harbor and think of the hardy sailors who have gone from the port on voyages of discovery and conquest. It has been claimed that they were the first to land at Guinea, at the Cape of Good Hope, and, in 1402, at the Canaries. The museum in the Hôtel de Ville should be visited for its collections of local antiquities, some of which

[53]

are from the Gallic camp, capable of holding thousands of men, which was situated about two miles from the present city. There are furniture, pictures, autographs, and many authentic reminders of the earlier day.

On the way to Puys we pass the château of the late Lord Salisbury and a cottage occupied by the younger Alexandre Dumas, author of "Camille." It was chiefly through Dumas that the place came to the attention of the Parisians as

NO, NOT A MODERN SILO, BUT AN ANCIENT
CASTLE AT DIEPPE

a resort. The harbor separates Dieppe from the suburb of Le Pollet, the home of fishermen, which is in direct contrast to the fashionable section of the watering-place. The inhabitants are a superstitious people, who tell about that terrible night when the sacristan heard the bell ringing and entered the Church of Notre Dame to find the priest at the altar and the congregation consisting of people long dead. During the mass, when the priest endeavored to raise the Host to his lips, it slipped from his fingers. Then he cried out to the sacristan: "My poor Peter, do you not recognize me? I am Regnaud, whose ship was wrecked on Monday in Easter week on the rock of Ailly. I had vowed a mass in honor of Our Lady and I forgot my vow. I try now to say this mass myself in order to keep my promise, but each time that I try to communicate, the Host escapes from my lips and I feel the torments of Hell in my bosom. Tell my son, I implore you,

MEDIEVAL KITCHEN AT THE MANOIR D'ANGO

never to forget the masses which he may promise to Our Lady!"

There are several excursions from Dieppe that are easily accomplished by motor-bus, and these should not be over-looked if one is driving a private car. The chief one, perhaps, is the historic Château d'Arques, reached in about fifteen minutes by railway. It was built by an uncle of William the Conqueror and was the last stronghold to fall into the hands of Philip Augustus when he took Normandy from King

BEAUVAIS: LOOKING TOWARD JEANNE HACHETTE'S STATUE IN CITY HALL SQUARE

John. Near by was fought the great battle that gave Henry of Navarre his victory over the Ligne.

Taking a motor at the Café de la Bourse, an attractive ride of less than three miles brings us to Varengeville and the Manoir d'Ango, a farmhouse built in the sixteenth century by the merchant prince Ango of Dieppe. Francis I was entertained in this old farmhouse. Entering the courtyard, we find it occupied by sheep and other domestic animals, and enclosed by the several buildings comprising the Manoir. Built in the style of the Renaissance, it is an architectural gem, elaborately carved, and with balconies and windows reminiscent of the Middle Ages. Time has left its imprint on the interior, and little remains of the original decorations. An old fireplace in the dining-room gives us some idea of the ornamentation, but the room is bare of furniture and is now used as a storage loft. The most interesting and best-preserved room is the kitchen, which is still used by the care-takers. It contains a large fireplace where kettles are hung over logs, and on either side are seats built in the brick-work, where the cook could watch the progress of the roast and other food in preparation for the table.

Farther along, half way to Havre, is Fécamp, with a rare old Abbey Church and a modern plant in which Benedictine cordial is made.

If you are going up from Dieppe to Paris, by all means stop off, midway, and see the ancient town of Beauvais, where skilled workmen are still making tapestries as beautiful as some of the old Gobelins that are treasured by museums. So delicate is this artistry in silk and wool that a skilled work-man is credited with good work if he weaves four square inches in a day. Beauvais Cathedral also is worth going far to see, with its magnificent south portal and lofty choir. The picturesque Place de l'Hôtel de Ville contains a bronze statue of Jean Hachette, a local heroine who led the women of Beauvais to victory in 1472 against Charles the Bold, and captured with her own hands a banner still preserved in the City Hall.

But if we have already seen Beauvais, let us wander from Dieppe north to St. Valéry-en-Caux and south along the Channel and into the heart of Normandy again. St. Valéry, a small seaside resort lying between great cliffs, is pretty but much less important than it was in the Middle Ages. It need not detain us long. The Norman countryside, however, is of perennial interest.

There is no mistaking the French atmosphere of the villages through which we travel. All have a style of archi-

CHALK CLIFFS OF ST. VALERY-EN-CAUX

A RICH MAN'S COUNTRY RESIDENCE NEAR ETRETAT

tecture and ornamentation peculiar to the country. The carved shop-fronts attract our attention. Many of these have considerable artistic merit; tho carved centuries ago, they are still an interesting feature of many of the cities of to-day.

We pass Norman farmhouses, quaint and pretty, usually surrounded by delightful shade trees; but they are seldom near the road. One may picture the quiet life these people lead, isolated from the great world. As a rule, the country is rolling, and at times we can see the road for several miles ahead of our car. Nearly every Norman roadway is lined on both sides by trees, which protect us from the direct rays of the sun. Rural homes are scattered, some the property of the farmer, others belonging to city merchants who have sought out a country home for the summer.

[59]

NATURE'S ORIGINAL FLYING BUTTRESS, NEAR ETRETAT

The fashionable watering-place of Etretat is of comparatively recent celebrity, as it was little more than a fishing village until the painter Isabey discovered it half a century or more ago and revealed its charms to the outside world, particularly to the artists and the composers, notably Courbet, Corot, Massenet, and Offenbach, all of whom found charm and inspiration here. The journalists of Paris were not far behind in sending enthusiastic accounts of the place to their newspapers and magazines, whereupon it suddenly became fashionable and popular in the summer months. The hotels and the Casino now are crowded during the season. The walk along the cliff to Côte d'Aval is to be recommended, because it affords one of the finest views of the coast; there are caves, natural arches, even a "flying buttress" in the sea, with numerous legends of interest to travelers.

There is the story of the three beautiful sisters who were
carried off by the Lord of Etretat, but declined to speak to
him. This so enraged him that he ordered them carried to
the top of the cliff and hurled from the precipice. After
that he was haunted by three phantoms until he died, which
anyone will admit was exactly as it should have been. Other
excursions are to Cap d'Antifer and its lighthouse, the Roc
aux Guillemots, Bruneval-les-Bains with its good bathing
beach, St. Jouin, Benouville and Yport, another fishing village that has become a favorite with the artists.

Deauville is the aristocratic twin of Trouville. It is con-
ceded that Trouville has the better beach, but Deauville,
especially at the time of the August races, is the most fashionable resort in northern France. Naturally, the stakes at
the Casino run high, as do the prices at the leading hotels.

DEAUVILLE'S FASHIONABLE CASINO BEFORE THE DAY'S
THRONG ARRIVES

ROYAL HOTEL AND GARDENS AT DEAUVILLE

Even at Easter the famous Terrasse de Deauville is one of the celebrated fashion promenades of Europe, and during certain weeks in summer is a spectacle worth seeing. Here are the Casino and the Baths on a fine sandy beach. The scene is brilliantly set off by tents, awnings, chairs, and other accessories of the modern bathing beach of the first class, reminding one of the Lido at Venice in August. The towns are almost deserted in the early summer, so far as visitors are concerned; but in July they assume a sudden life and are more Parisian than Paris itself. Here milady changes her frock several times a day for the promenade or public appearance, and each time a change is made it is supposed to denote progress toward the climax, which is likely to be the latest mode from the creators of style at Paris. The Casino opens on June 15, and naturally is the pivot of the gay world's movements. There are the customary amusements of such resorts: races, dramas, concerts, dances. The regattas attract crowds of French and English visitors in August, and during the same month the races are of considerable interest. The first fortnight is supposed to make a special appeal to the professional followers of the game; the last two weeks, which end in the Grand Prix de Deauville, are particularly attractive to the fashionable world. Trouville races have been compared with the Epsom meeting in England, and Deauville with Ascot.

In the days of the Duc de Morny, who founded Deauville during the Second Empire, and for many years after that during the period of crinolines and Dundrearys, the hill overlooking the town was the favorite promenade from Deauville. It was the fashion, a recent writer tells us, to mount

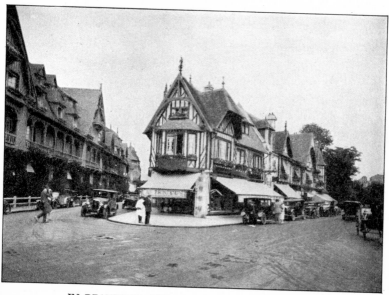

IN DEAUVILLE, NEAR THE HOTEL NORMANDY

the slope past the quaint priory of Starncult to the ruins of
the Château du Lassay, where the air is like wine and one gets
the sweeping panorama over the valley of the Touques, with
Havre in the distance glittering magnificently. The new
Golf Hotel Club is placed not far from these ruined walls, all
that is left of the château, which is said to have been built in
a few weeks by the Grande Mademoiselle as a place to receive
her cousin, King Louis. The hotel itself, with its spacious
rooms, verandas and apartments permitting an uninterrupted
view of the wooded valley and the sea, is now an ideal resort
for the golfer.

There are two splendid churches in Deauville that should
attract more admiration than they doubtless do from visitors;
for it is safe to assume that the mind of the stranger in Deauville or Trouville is not concerned with religious practises,

ENJOYING LIFE ON THE SANDS OF TROUVILLE

ST. ETIENNE, CAEN, FOUNDED BY
WILLIAM THE CONQUEROR

nor with architecture. Notre Dame des Victoires has a marble altar from the ruins of Pompeii and some worthwhile frescoes. Notre Dame de Bon Secours is the other church that should be seen. One directing the route of a private motor car will find many pleasing excursions in the vicinity; and there are many roadways that beckon to the pedestrian, who finds enchanting landscapes along the route. It is an eighteen-mile journey to Lisieux; and a very pleasant ride along the route is from Trouville to Caen, by way of Houlgate and Cabourg. Both of these latter villages are popular with American and English travelers, many of them lingering here a few days before sailing for home from one of the near-by ports. Handsome châteaux are being built in this district in increasing numbers, and some of them are rented (completely furnished) for as much as three thousand dollars for the three summer months.

TRINITY CHURCH, CAEN, BUILT
BY THE CONQUEROR'S WIFE

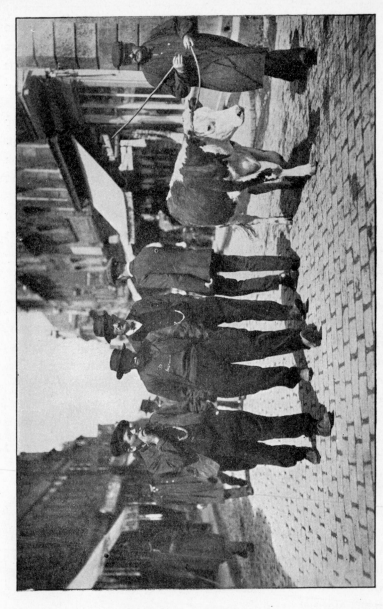

PEASANTS ON THE WAY TO MARKET AT VIRE

On a quiet country road near Trouville we are startled to come upon a vicious looking dog, apparently ready to attack us; but our fears vanish when we discover that the brute is only a porcelain likeness. In a neighboring house is the factory where such animals, birds, and reptiles are made—and made to look remarkably like their originals. The top of the house resembles a menagerie at large, while the lawn is covered with so many specimens of walking and crawling creatures that only a total abstainer would feel safe among them.

Situated on the river Orne is Caen, which next to Rouen is the largest and most important city in Normandy. Its streets are filled with excellent examples of medieval architecture, and it also contains several fine Gothic churches, beautiful and of great historic interest. Among the finest is St. Etienne, founded by William the Conqueror in 1062. This church, while far simpler in style than La Trinité, built by his wife, is much grander in proportion. It is an expression in stone of the imperial will of the conquering Duke, while the other breathes the true spirit of his loving and faithful Duchess. La Trinité was built in the same year as St. Etienne, and is much richer, more delicate in workmanship. One is the emanation of the masculine, the other a design of the feminine mind, but both are noble examples of the early Gothic.

St. Etienne, or the Abbaye aux Hommes, was intended by the Conqueror as a resting-place for his own remains, and it was finished and dedicated to him during his lifetime. A marble slab in the pavement before the high altar marks the grave of William, which was violated by the Huguenots and the Revolutionists and has been empty for a long time. In the sacristy is an old portrait of the Conqueror that dates

CLOCK TOWER AT VIRE

from the fifteenth or sixteenth century. The Abbaye aux Dames, or La Trinité, was part of a vow to perform some good work as a result of the papal dispensation which countenanced the marriage of William and Mathilde, his first cousin. At the time of the dedication, their little daughter was consecrated as the first abbess.

Across from this church is St. Giles, now much restored. It was a mortuary chapel for the burial of the poor and contains some twelfth-century work. The principal parish church of Caen is St. Pierre. The spire and tower, which date from 1308, have been called "the best examples of a class of spire which, built upon one general principle, seems to have been dispersed through a considerable district around Caen, tho not a great number remain without mutilations and several are still incomplete. Of these, the church of St. Pierre offers the best-known example." There are several ecclesiastical edifices of former importance, some of which have been altered almost beyond recognition.

The University of Caen was founded in 1436, but the earliest of the existing buildings dates from 1701. The museum in the Hôtel de Ville should be visited for its pictures and library. Here we find Van Dyck's "Portrait of a Young Man," Van der Helst's "Portrait of a Woman," Rubens's "Melchisedec Offering Bread to Abraham," Carpaccio's "Madonna and Child," Perugino's "Marriage of the Virgin," and several other masterpieces, including "Jesus Crowned with Thorns," attributed to Ribera and sometimes to Van Dyck. The library has one hundred thousand volumes, and valuable fifteenth and sixteenth century manuscripts. A Museum of Antiquities has many interesting items. A pleasant ramble may be taken around the city in search of old houses and other buildings.

Some of the guide-books suggest a week's stay at Caen, but this is good advice only for one who has the leisure; the American traveling in Normandy, however, should remain at least a couple of days. Madame de Sévigné wrote of the town in the eighteenth century: "That is the prettiest town, the most inviting, the gayest, the best-placed; it has the handsomest streets, the finest buildings, the most beautiful churches, meadows, walks," and to an extent her high praise is appropriately incorporated in a description of the present city.

Leaving Caen we ride to Vire, where we arrive on market day. The streets of the village are crowded with peasants, who have brought with them their domestic animals, hoping to sell them. Men and women leading cows and horses, or dragging pigs, are on their way to the market-place. The peasants are of the old Norman type; their ancestors lived here, and generation after generation comes and goes, few of them ever leaving their native home. Here we find none of the excitable people of the large cities; it is a simple and peaceful community, engaged in agricultural pursuits, content to live as did its ancestors.

The age of the castle on the hill is unknown; a portion of the ruins stands in a public garden with pretty walks that reach to the water's edge. At one time the rural old town was surrounded by walls and was considered of sufficient importance to become a King's ransom, when Edward III demanded it for the release of King John. One of its chief sights to-day is the famous clock-tower, the lower portion of which belongs to the thirteenth century and doubtless was attached to the fortifications. There is a cupola and a statue of the Virgin and not far away is the church of Notre Dame.

IV LISIEUX AND ROUEN

LISIEUX, ON THE TOUQUES RIVER, HAS MUCH TO DELIGHT THE ARTISTIC EYE

IV

LISIEUX AND ROUEN

LISIEUX has attracted visitors for centuries. They came to see the city's beautiful churches and splendid old houses, which are more remarkable than the similar edifices of Chester in England that have fascinated world travelers. In recent years, however, the visitors have become far more numerous. Where there were hundreds, there are now tens of thousands. Instead of a few curious tourists, there are now trainloads of pilgrims—devout believers in Thérèse, the Little Flower of Jesus, one of the most recent of canonized saints in the Roman Catholic Church, whose fame has spread with remarkable rapidity to the ends of the earth, and who in a few years has gained a following among the devout barely equaled by other saints of history.

Marie Françoise Thérèse Martin, ninth child of Louis Martin and his wife, was born at Lisieux on January 2, 1873. To-day, a tablet on the balcony of 42 Rue St. Blaise informs the faithful of that auspicious event. She came of a deeply religious family, several members of which were in convents; and when she was sixteen years of age, she also entered the Carmel, where she remained until September 30, 1897, when she died. An ecclesiastical tribunal was convened by the Bishop of Bayeux to examine the cause of Sister Thérèse, of the Child Jesus, and of the Holy Face. The tribunal sent a copy of its findings to the Prefect of the Sacred Congrega-

NO WONDER PILGRIMS LOVE THE HOME TOWN OF ST. THERESE!

tion of Rites at Rome, after having taken the depositions of forty-five witnesses and having studied a huge mass of correspondence from every country in Europe, as well as from distant parts of the world, all declaring emphatically that she who had promised to "come down from heaven" had fulfilled her promise and had wrought many miracles. She also had said: "I shall spend my heaven in doing good on earth." This episcopal process, or inquiry into the virtues, miracles, and reputation for holiness of one who has died in "the odor of sanctity," always precedes the Apostolic or Roman Process. The title of "Venerable" accompanies the introduction of the Process in Rome. Ten years are supposed to elapse between the two inquiries; but this delay was suppressed in favor of Sister Thérèse, and her cause made rapid progress toward beatification and final canonization.

Rarely in history has there been such an appeal from the entire world.

In 1910 the body was exhumed; the remains were placed in a leaden coffin and sealed. On the cover a plate was soldered, bearing the words: "Soeur Thérèse de l'Enfant Jesu et de la Saint Face. Marie Françoise Thérèse Martin, 1873-1897." The same inscription was duplicated upon a copper plate fixed to the outer oak coffin and it was lowered into a grave not far removed from the first and lined with bricks.

Afterwards, the pilgrimages increased. The Carmel received tens of thousands of letters from all parts of the world, and these continue to arrive in a never-ceasing stream. The faithful of all nations write to tell of the blessings received through the intercession of the Little Flower. Statues and paintings of her have been erected in the churches

CARMELITE CHURCH AND SHRINE OF ST. THERESE IN LISIEUX

of Christendom. Perhaps she is named oftener in the petitions and prayers of the faithful than almost any single one of the saints. And there is a natural desire to visit the scene of her earthly pilgrimage. Travelers who go to Lisieux nowadays think more of the grave of the Little Flower and of other places associated with her brief life than of the history of the city, its beautiful churches, and its picturesque secular buildings.

Remains of ancient houses indicate that the inhabitants of Lisieux were rich at one time, and that the whole city enjoyed a period of great prosperity, followed by a period of slower growth. Its changed fortune to-day reminds one of Bruges in Belgium.

Lisieux was the Gallo-Roman city of Noviomagus, which became the seat of a bishop in the sixth century. The boule-

A BACK-DOOR VISTA IN LISIEUX

vards of to-day follow the lines of the fortifications of the fifteenth century. Pierre Cauchon, remembered because he was the accuser of Jeanne d'Arc, was bishop of Lisieux in 1432. King Richard of England had a famous interview with his rebellious brother John at Lisieux. Upon their meeting, John fell down at Richard's feet. "You are but a child," said the King, "and you have been in bad company. It is they who shall pay for what you have done."

WHERE THE SEINE MEANDERS DOWN
THROUGH NORMANDY

Probably the chief architectural gem of the city is the Parish Church of St. Pierre, formerly the Cathedral, which stands at the end of the market-place and is approached by broad steps. It is contemporary with the Cathedral of Canterbury and is the oldest Gothic church in Normandy. The western towers and nave are of the twelfth century, the spire of the southern tower is of seventeenth-century work, and the nave chapels and the Lady Chapel date from the fifteenth century. The southwestern porch has been described by John Ruskin in the "Seven Lamps of Architecture." The Lady Chapel is the work of Cauchon, who in the deed of endowment mentions that he built the chapel in atonement for his "false judgment in condemning an innocent woman." It was in this church that Henry II married Eleanor of Guyenne. One of the interesting old customs of the Cathedral is recorded by Ducarel, writing in 1750.

"The canons of this church, by virtue of a compact be-

NORMANDY IS FULL OF ATTRACTIVE RURAL HOMES

tween them and the bishop," he writes, "enjoy the extraordinary privilege of being Earls of Lisieux, with the full exercise of all civil and criminal jurisdiction within the earldom, during the vigil and feast-day of St. Ursinus in every year (i. e., the tenth and eleventh of June). In order to perpetuate this right, two of the canons elected by the chapter for that purpose, having on the vigil of the saint dressed themselves in their surplices, covered with bandoleers of flowers and holding nosegays in their hands, mount on horseback at the great door of the Cathedral, and ride to each of the four gates of the city, preceded by two mace-bearers, two chaplains, and twenty-five halberdiers armed with helmets and cuirasses, and followed by all the officers of justice on horseback, clothed in their proper habits, covered with bandoleers of flowers and carrying nosegays in their hands. As soon as these canons arrive at the city

"TRADE IS SLOW TO-DAY"

gates, the keys are delivered up to them, and they there post a proper guard of their own, in lieu of that of the archbishop, which on the delivery of the keys to the canons, immediately marches out. All customs payable within the city, and the profits of the fair therein, held on St. Ursinus day, belong to those two canonical Earls: in consideration of which, they deliver to each of the other canons a loaf of bread and two flagons of wine, and in case any post or place of profit within the earldom becomes vacant during these two days, they have the sole right of nomination and presentation thereunto."

The former bishop's palace adjoins the Cathedral and now houses the law courts, the library and the museum, the latter containing paintings and antiquities. The gardens of the palace have been called "the finest public gardens in France." Under the chestnut and lime trees are groups of statues, some of which are casts from the antique. The village of Val

[79]

OLD TIMBERED HOUSES IN ROUEN, ON ONE OF THE CITY'S MANY PICTURESQUE STREETS

Richer, once notable for its abbey, of which Thomas à Becket
was the first abbot, is near by. It was to this abbey that
Becket retired on his exile from England, and some of his
vestments are still shown. It seems likely that he resided also
in the palace at Lisieux.

The most important city in Normandy is Rouen, the name
of which prompts many memories. Let us go there directly
from Lisieux—each a city associated closely with the life of a
saint: Rouen with Jeanne d'Arc, who saved her country from
the tyranny of an earthly foe; Lisieux with Sainte Thérèse,
who gave her life to "pray France back from sin and unbelief."

We find Rouen a thoroughly modern city, busily engaged
in weaving, spinning, and the manufacture of handkerchiefs.
But that is not why thousands of Americans enter its gates
every year, and even find the time to stop off for a few hours
in the quick journey from the ports of arrival to Paris.
Rouen is fascinating to the tourist because it is "a museum of
antiquities" and because it recalls tragic memories of Jeanne
d'Arc. The national and civic governments have given
thoughtful care to Rouen's treasures, guarding them jealously
for future generations.

Perhaps we can do no better, after arrival, than to pay our
first visit to the Museum of Antiquities, where we shall gain
an impression of the city that was. This museum will give
us a needed perspective for forming an adequate opinion of
the splendid city, which, when casually viewed by the new-
comer, seems so hustling and modern. Here are numerous
carvings, pillars, and façades rescued from old buildings that
have resigned in favor of modern progress.

Close to two thousand years ago, Rouen was Rotomagus,
capital of a Roman province, and of great importance even

STONE MARKING THE SPOT WHERE
JOAN OF ARC WAS BURNED

then. It had an eventful history down through the ages, being pillaged, sacked, and burned, rebuilt and then again destroyed. It was ravaged in religious wars. It was occupied by the Germans in 1870, and then again it loomed in importance when the British Expeditionary Force came in 1914; still later it became a center for the Army Service Corps and base hospitals. Several of the great military cemeteries are situated here, it being declared that there are over fifteen thousand graves in St. Sever alone.

But let us put aside all thought of the Rouen of to-day as we visit some of its monuments and review their association with great events of history. First of all, we are interested in anything connected with the life and death of the national heroine, Jeanne d'Arc. Let us go to the old castle of Philip Augustus and recall that after her victories, the poor maid of Domremy arrived here on a bleak afternoon of December, 1430. For weeks, while the spineless King who could have saved her was wasting his time at Chinon, she lay in her dark dungeon, and her judges, who had been chosen from her bitterest enemies, "sought accusation against her to put her to death." In the structure we see the instruments of torture with which she was threatened, if she would not confess to heresy. And we imagine that we hear her reply:

"If you should tear me limb from limb until my soul part

company from my body, I can say no more than I have said. And even if, forced by pain, I should say something else, afterwards I should always declare that you made me say it by force."

We return to the city by the Rue Jeanne d'Arc to the Rue Saint-Romain, where a tablet on the Archbishop's Palace informs us that here took place the final trial, when she was excommunicated and given over to her merciless foes. We then go to the Gros Horloge or Clock Tower built in 1389. Jeanne d'Arc came this way at the last because it led through the gate to the place of execution. In the market-place we find the slab that marks the site of the scaffold on which the wood was piled, ready for lighting. The fire is kindled and the flames close around her body! It all took place five hundred years ago, but the scene seems to be reenacted, if we

GROS HORLOGE OR CLOCK TOWER IN ROUEN

[83]

ROUEN SEEN FROM THE TOP OF THE SUSPENSION BRIDGE

THE PALACE OF JUSTICE IN ROUEN

have imaginative minds. The
secretary of the English King
cries: "We are lost, we are
lost, for a saint has been
burned to death this day!"

Recalling that cry, let us
go to the Church of Notre
Dame, in which a splendid
chapel has been erected to
Jeanne, close to the place of
her martyrdom. It is considered one of the finest churches
in France and was begun in
the year 1201. The famous
Butter Tower, a fine example
of the Flamboyant style, was

AN OLD CANAL IN ROUEN

erected in the fifteenth century and paid for by the issuance
of indulgences to eat butter during Lent. The edifice is
over four hundred and fifty feet long. We observe the
stained glass in the nave and transepts, and there is a fine
rose-window in the western front, part of which dates from
the sixteenth century. The choir is a pure example of the
thirteenth-century style and contains nearly one hundred
carved stalls. The heart of Richard I of England is interred
beneath an effigy in the ambulatory. The Lady Chapel contains fine tombs of two cardinals and has numerous statues.
The trade-guilds have several small chapels, and a splendid
collection of tapestries is displayed here on feast days. On the
north side is a tomb erected in 1541 by the notorious Diane
de Poitiers, mistress of Henry II, in memory of her husband.

The Church of St. Ouen is considered finer and is larger than
the Cathedral. It is likely that the present edifice is the fifth

ST. OUEN CHURCH, ROUEN, A SUPERB EXAMPLE OF
PURE GOTHIC ARCHITECTURE

or sixth that has occupied the site. It dates from the fourteenth to the sixteenth centuries. The tower has been called
"exquisite, fairylike, a gem of architecture" and dates from
the fifteenth century. The church is over four hundred feet
long, one hundred feet high and eighty feet wide. The world
regards it as an almost perfect example of the Flamboyant
style, and sometimes as "a culminating triumph of Gothic
architecture." It also has considerable historic interest,
because the so-called rite of abjuration, during which Jeanne
d'Arc was brought to abjure her mission, was conducted here.
Charles VIII of France held a reception here, when he confirmed the charters of the city. Henry VII of England was a
member of his suite at the time.

From here we go to the Church of St. Maclou, named for a

Scotchman, who became a bishop in the sixth century and whose shrine was erected at Rouen. The western front is rich in ornamentation. The chief treasures are the carved doors and organ staircase. After studying the former, Ruskin was moved to write one of his poetical descriptions. The Church of St. Vivien should be observed, chiefly on account of its square towers and octagonal spire, which date from the fourteenth century. Next, we go to the Chapelle de la Fierté de St. Romain. It is small and was built for what was known as the Privilège de St. Romain ceremony, which lasted from the thirteenth to the eighteenth century. It was a privilege exercised by the canons of the Cathedral and consisted of the release of a condemned criminal on Ascension Day. The legend is that St. Romain, a patron saint of Rouen, taking with him a condemned criminal, started out to free the country from a fearful dragon. The saint returned to Rouen, the criminal leading the dragon by a rope made from the bishop's stole. The dragon was so overcome by piety that the criminal found no difficulty in pushing him into the river, where he was drowned, and thus Rouen was freed from fear. It has been said by certain skeptical critics that the ceremony existed before the legend, and that the latter was created to give it religious significance.

ELABORATE GOTHIC PORTAL OF
ST. MACLOU, ROUEN

[87]

WHERE BENEDICTINE CORDIAL IS MADE—AT FECAMP
ON THE ENGLISH CHANNEL

Let us go to the Place de la Pucelle to visit the Hôtel du Bourgtheroulde, a notable example of the transition from Gothic to Renaissance architecture, dating from the beginning of the sixteenth century. The famous meeting in 1520 between the kings of France and England is commemorated on a series of carved panels. There are also panels representing Petrarch's Triumphs. The Palais de Justice is a splendid late-Gothic building, which is now occupied by the law courts. It is the finest secular building in the city.

Rouen is another city in which the tourist will find it to his advantage to remain for a few days, after the principal points of interest in the town itself have been exhausted. There is a fine modern hotel where one may live in comfort during a visit of any length.

V FASCINATING BRITTANY

DINARD, BRITTANY'S FAVORITE SEASIDE RESORT

V

FASCINATING BRITTANY

OPPOSITE St. Malo is Dinard, a fashionable watering-place which we reach by ferry. Placing our motor-car on the ferry-boat, we cross the bay and ascend a steep road to the town. Dinard is now the leading bathing resort in Brittany because of its attractive site, its spacious, sandy beach, pleasant walks, and superb views. Its environs are liberally sprinkled with villas, many of them the property of the English.

An hour's ride brings us to Dinan, an interesting Breton town, with a number of old buildings, lovely flower-gardens, odd-looking streets, and quaint people. It is an old walled town with about six thousand inhabitants, which, like so many of the French cities, has had its day in the sun. Orig-inally it was a feudal lordship, and in the fourteenth century, by agreement, its fate was staked upon a duel between a French and an English champion. At the time of the War of American Independence, a regiment of Irish rebels in the French service was quartered there. Two churches and the castle are the chief sights of the town, but it is here that we obtain our introduction to the picturesque Bretons, who still retain their ancient costumes, and have not lost faith in their legends nor love for their native land.

Legends are often souvenirs of actual events, and if we remove the embroideries in which the popular imagination has wrapped them, we shall frequently discover facts of great

DINAN'S MEDIEVAL RAMPARTS

interest. It is never safe to despise a legend, especially in so poetic a land as Brittany. If we take from the poor women working in a typical Breton laundry, their legends and fairy tales, we deprive them of their greatest comforter. They work in the fields and till the soil; but few of them are supplied with modern machinery, or even know much about it.

One day when we were in Brittany a horse attached to a cart, in which there was an old Breton woman fast asleep, took fright and ran away, overturning the cart. We found the poor old lady in the roadway in the midst of her purchases, while the horse was still careering off in the distance. All she could say was, "How could you be such a bad beast!" But when we offered to take her home in our motor-car, nothing would induce her to enter it. She said she had heard of these monsters, which were only fit for Satan and his crew to ride in, not for a Christian who went to mass every Sunday.

The farmers' homes are neither pretentious nor luxurious. One seldom finds an unkempt interior, and as a rule the house is surrounded by a garden. Rooms are not plentiful, usually not more than three; sometimes but two, a kitchen and a living and dining room combined. Entering one of the homes, we saw five carved-oak sleeping-places that lined the

[92]

walls. Our hostess, pointing to a nook beside the fireplace, explained:

"My husband and I sleep there, my father next to us, then my brother, and beyond, my servant, with the children. This bed by the window, we keep for visitors. Have you beds in America?"

I reassured her on that point, but explained that it was our custom to sleep in separate rooms.

"But how lonely!" she said; "we would not dare to sleep so; here we protect one another."

Dol is a strange little town that seems to have been overlooked by the present-day world, because its old houses and stodgy inhabitants seem wholly unaware of passing events in the outside world. Decay is everywhere, and someone has imagined that "ghosts walk of nights in its cobbled main

PRIMITIVE FARM METHODS IN THIS CORNER OF FRANCE

DOL STILL PRESERVES ITS QUAINT MEDIEVAL HOUSES

street." There is a legend of a battle that took place here, after which sufficient blood flowed to turn a mill-wheel; and in the midst of the fray, two brothers caught hold of one another by the throat and a huge stone arose out of the earth to separate them—all of which is supposed to account for the Great Menhir of Dol, which remains to prove the truth of the story. It is likely that Dol was a place of considerable religious importance in the pre-Christian era. It stood in the middle of a mighty and mysterious forest, from whose oaks the Druids gathered mistletoe; but the forest was submerged by the ocean, which threatened to include the town. Samson, a former Archbishop of York, who had fled from England and become the first Bishop of Dol, came to the rescue and as an answer to his prayer the town was saved. The forest, however, was swept into the sea and, according to the legend, took root on the islands of Jersey and Guernsey. Samson became the favorite saint of Dol, and the fine Cathedral is dedicated to him. It was here that Châteaubriand attended school before he went to college at Dinan.

The Cathedral is chiefly of the thirteenth century, and it possesses several English characteristics. A pleasant excursion of not more than four miles brings us to Mont Dol, which rises about two hundred feet, a bold, granite rock, surmounted by a modern chapel. It probably was a Druid center, and in Roman times the site of a temple to Cybele or perhaps to Diana. Several of the popular saints and apostles of Brittany were associated with it, and it is represented in the Bayeux tapestry. On one of the rocks is a footprint of St. Michel, made when he left for Mont St. Michel.

As we pass through St. Brieux, on either side of us are the

ONE OF THE MANY PREHISTORIC DOLMENS IN BRITTANY

familiar washing-pools, which one sees everywhere in Brittany; and scattered over the grass-covered hillside, which looks like a snowstorm in summer, is the household linen of the entire community. The town is not likely to detain us, for altho it has had a notable history, there is not much remaining to hold our interest. It is very picturesque, however, and one who goes on walking tours in the region may conveniently make it a stopping-place. One who desires to

WASH-DAY ON THE OUTSKIRTS OF ST. BRIEUX

study the spectacular fisher-folk may do so in this neighborhood.

Guingamp, a quaint old name and a quaint old town, is fascinating because it is so out-of-date and antiquated. The goods in the dull shops have probably not been renewed since the days of Duchesse Anne. Only on Sundays and religious holidays do the streets awaken from their lethargy. As we pass the church we glance into the north porch, crowded as ever with country women praying and offering their devotions to the miraculous statue of Notre Dame de Bon Secours, which, clad in gorgeous robes, stands high above the inner doors. The Pardon of Notre Dame or the Festival of Fire, which takes place here in July, brings people from many parts of the country. Thousands of pilgrims carrying candles, singing as they march through the streets, seem like a procession of white-capped cherubs of all ages. The air grows thick with the smell of burnt wax, and the great Festival of Fire is on in earnest. Bonfires are lighted around poles, from the tops of which stream banners bearing the inscription, "Ave Maria!" Around the doors of the church are pictures of the saints and the Madonna. The bells ring and the people hurry about the streets, going to and from the Cathedral and passing the booths, shooting galleries, shows, and buffets along

GOING TO CHURCH ON A SUNDAY MORNING

[97]

THE STATELY ARCHES OF THE VIADUCT ADD TO THE BEAUTY OF MORLAIX

the way. Most of the natives are dressed in fantastic costumes, the girls in white coifs, bright aprons, and their finest
dresses; and the boys and young men in jackets embroidered
in silver, and mushroom-shaped hats with velvet streamers.
They promenade, laugh, and sing. "Pardon," for them, is
not merely a religious festival; it is also a time for making
merry, a sort of carnival or fair. It is said that in all Brittany
there is nothing more reminiscent of the Middle Ages than
this celebration, altho there are many "Pardons" in other
towns.

From Guingamp we go to Morlaix, which almost everyone
knows. Its picturesque confusion of market, shipping, and
beggars is all dominated and dwarfed by the great viaduct
that crosses the deep valley. The old streets have a charm,
dark and winding as they are, for there are strange corners
and quaint interiors teeming with interest. As we look at
these old houses, years fade away, and from the doorways
come men and women of the Middle Ages. Even the vendors
in the streets interest us; they are of an unfamiliar type, these
white-capped Bretons, an inspiration for the brush of an
artist. Good wholesome faces, honest and hard-working
people. It is said that the Fontaine des Anglais marks the
spot where six hundred English were caught asleep, after an
attack upon the town, and promptly slain. There are some
fine old timbered houses in the town, and there is one church
worth visiting—that of St. Melaine, which dates from the
fifteenth century.

It is but a short journey from here to Saint Jean du Doigt,
and as we near it the ground seems to melt from beneath us.
Down we go, past little houses and granite crosses, into a
deep green velvet ravine, where, amid purple cliffs, is the
Church of St. John. Within the churchyard is the miracu-

CHURCH OF ST. JEAN-DU-DOIGT

lous fountain where Duchesse Anne came to be cured of an affliction of the eyes. In gratitude for her recovery, she lavished many costly gifts upon this shrine, and they may still be seen in the sacristy.

The great "Pardon" occurs here on June 21 each year—another spectacular celebration, which attracts many believers and crowds of visitors. There are beggars galore, and many lame and blind, all craving miraculous relief from their condition. At the principal service of the day, a sermon is preached, with the chief religious relic of the place as the subject—the miraculous finger of St. John the Baptist, which has given its modern name to the village and brought it fame. Formerly the town was called Traoun-Meriadek, the town above which the Sacred Fire had been lighted, but it was destined for even greater honors.

St. John's finger had been the property of the Church of St. Jean du Day, in Normandy. There was a Breton in service there at about the time of Jeanne d'Arc's exploits. He was returning to his native village, and he wanted to take along something of great value, which suggested the idea of obtaining the sacred finger for his own parish church. He went to the church where it reposed in a reliquary and prayed fervently, after which he felt a mysterious calm and satisfaction, altho he did not know the reason.

On his homeward journey, he observed that trees waved their branches as he passed beneath them; bells in the villages through which he passed, suddenly began to ring, altho the buildings were unoccupied. The inhabitants of one of these villages became terrified and rushed from their houses to ascertain the cause of the mysterious happenings; but as they found only a travel-stained Breton boy, they locked him in the jail and charged him with disturbing their peace. He fell asleep in the prison; but when he awakened, he had been transported to a hillside near his native village. And strangely enough, the bells in the church began to ring as he approached and found the congregation assembled for mass. It seemed to him that the palm of his right hand opened, and altho no blood came from the wound, something came out of it, flew to the choir and dropped upon the cloth of the high altar, after which the candles flamed up. The finger of St. John the Baptist had lodged in his hand, as an answer to his prayers, and he had not been aware of it until he reached the church in his village.

A SERIOUS LITTLE BRETON MAID

A new church was built on the site, and the place quickly became a shrine that attracted the faithful from all parts of the country. It became popular to attend the "Pardon" by boat, and hundreds of small craft made a veritable

ST. THEGONNEC BOASTS A HANDSOME RENAISSANCE CHURCH

flotilla that set out from the Haven of Leon Tregor, following a fishing-boat that was garlanded with flowers and bore a cross at the top of its mast.

At Pointe de Primel is the seashore, now a bathing beach. This northern coast of Brittany has been a great haunt of dragons, and there are many chapels dedicated to Saint Michel, the Prince of dragon-slayers.

We visit St. Thégonnec with its well-known church, so extensive and ornate that, as we approach it, the triumphal arch forming its entrance appears to us like the gateway to some splendid monastery. It is a striking example of Renaissance architecture out of all proportion to the tiny village of which it is the pride. In the center of the graveyard rises a graceful Calvary. In this vicinity the people are so religious that they consider themselves disgraced if a priest is not a member of their family. As we meet the attractive residents of this little village, we see in their faces indications of peace and contentment; the freshness of youth is the treasured possession of most of the girls. Near by is the village of Landivisiau, with its ancient fountain, the back of which is formed of a number of panels carved in relief, probably taken from one of the demolished churches. It is dedicated to Saint Tivisiau. It is a privilege to meet the charming girls who make their homes in these Breton villages. This is the only part of France where the peasants retain their ancient costumes; a simple, home-loving people, whose affability makes our visit among them a delight.

Nowhere is the garb of the women quainter than at Plougastel, which is noted for the beautiful costumes of its inhabitants. At one time a terrible pestilence broke out here, and

THE CURIOUS OLD CALVARY AT PLOUGASTEL

[103]

TO HAVE AND TO HOLD

the people vowed if they were delivered from it they would erect a calvary as a token of gratitude. The plague was stayed, and true to their promise the calvary was built. It is massive, and bears on its platform a number of granite figures in a scene from the life of Jesus. In most of these villages the cemetery lies in the very heart of the town; it is the playground of the children, the meeting-place of lovers, the favorite spot for the old ladies, and a haven where the men-folk smoke their evening pipes. They like to have their dead where they can watch their graves from their windows, and pass them every time they go to church. "If we bury them away from the village, the dead will neither hear the singing nor the services," they explain. As we look at groups of the kindly peasant-folk of Plougastel, we see in their faces the childlike appearance that indicates a love for fairy-story and legend. They are the kind of men and women who never grow old. The "Pardon" takes place here on June 24 and popularly is known as the "Pardon of the Birds," the pilgrims bringing a great variety of birds in cages when they attend the services in the church.

Not far distant is the village of Châteaulin, which owes its existence to the important slate-quarries in the vicinity. We are now in one of the most interesting parts of Brittany, where myths, fables, and legends are woven into the very existence of the people. Le Faou is the starting point for Rumengol when the "Pardon" is held there. It is an odd little village with quaint buildings lining the one street in the town. The same costume which has been worn for centuries is still retained. We find the little girls particularly attractive, clad in the characteristic Breton outfit, their tiny bonnets black in place of the conventional white which we have become accustomed to seeing on the older women.

Away to the right, in a beautifully rounded valley, is Rumengol, the scene of another "Pardon" held in June, which I recently attended. Ominous-looking clouds overhung the valley that June day, causing one of us to remark that it was going to rain. The old caretaker, shocked at our heretical statement, turned to us and said: "You need not have the slightest anxiety; the weather of the Blessed Virgin

A BRETON BRIDE AND GROOM

[105]

of Rumengol is proverbial; it never rains at the time of the Pardon. How could it? It would spoil thousands of beautiful gowns."

The legend of Rumengol is more elaborate than some of the others, but it is quaint and typical of the district. It explains the "Pardon of the Singers" and why it is that so

WEDDING GUESTS IN FULL REGALIA

many lusty voices are raised in song here during the celebration. King Granlon, at the command of a monk, cast his daughter into the sea, so that the rest of the occupants of a boat might be saved from drowning. The sea suddenly became calm, and the King and his party reached the land in safety. The King, however, was haunted by the sound of his daughter's cries as she was swallowed by the waves; but his spiritual adviser told him to praise God for saving his own life.

The monarch went to live with the monks in the Abbey of Landevennec, and one night he heard beautiful sing-ing. Crossing to the window, he looked out over the sea and recognized the head and shoulders of his daughter above the waves. She was singing a seductive song, sim-ilar to that with which the

A CHURCH DOOR IN BRITTANY

Lorelei on the Rhine lured men to destruction, and he recognized his own child as the beautiful creature, half-fish, half-woman, whose song caused men to dive into the sea and whose kisses were so poisonous that her victims died imme-diately her lips had touched them.

When the King was about to die, he told a Druid that his last wish was to found a church—on the spot where he lay—to the Sorrowful Mother of God, so that the sick and weary might come to the shrine to pray. When the King reached Paradise, according to the legend, he met the Mother of Jesus, who thanked him for the church he had built in her honor and inquired whether he had a request to make of her. He replied in the affirmative, and implored her to prevent his daughter from singing and luring men to destruction. She replied that she could not do this, but that she would give others the power to sing more sweetly than the siren, so that the unholy charm of the latter would be broken. Thus at the time of the "Pardon" all voices of the devout are raised in

[107]

song—even at the vigil in the churchyard, when lanterns illumine the faces of the worshipers. Sometimes a girl who possesses a good voice is selected to stand beneath the calvary and sing—a survival, perhaps, of ancient rites in which a Druid priestess conducted the service.

VI FROM QUIMPER TO QUIBERON

A CHARMING VIEW IN THE HEART OF QUIMPER

VI

FROM QUIMPER TO QUIBERON

AFTER we had started for Quimper, we stopped the motor-car to watch a crowd of peasants, who were dancing on the highway. Two musicians blew lustily on a clarinet and a bagpipe, while the villagers went through the intricate figures of a Breton national dance. It was an unusually joyous occasion, and all were attired in their very best, a variety of gorgeous costumes resplendent in color and beautifully embroidered. Singing as they danced, they made a spectacle worth watching.

Most conspicuous were a bride and groom, the center of a delighted group of guests who were making merry at their wedding. We regretted that we had missed the ceremony, but our disappointment was only momentary, as we learned that in Brittany a certain day is set aside for weddings, and that no less than four couples were to be married in this little village that afternoon. We remained to witness the marriage ceremony and then rode along to Quimper, where we arrived just in time to see another wedding procession walking through the streets of the town. It was a different kind of wedding, however; the others had been weddings of country folk, but this was a sailor's wedding. It is said of the Breton sailor, as of others, that he has a sweetheart in every port, and we wondered whether the smiling and trusting bride was just another added to the jolly tar's list.

Quimper is a pleasant riverside city of fables and gables,

[111]

"THE SAILOR'S WIFE THE SAILOR'S STAR SHALL BE"

one of the best known and most popular places in Brittany. No visitor to France should omit this charming place from his itinerary. It lies about ten miles from the sea, yet it is a port; it boasts a small harbor on the Odet, along the banks of which we see many picturesque washerwomen. Quimper is an unusually interesting town on market days, when the country folk bring their produce to the Grande Place—even to the steps of the church itself—and bedecked seemingly for a masquerade ball, offer ducks, geese, fruits, and vegetables for sale. We may find it amusing to count the number of different coifs worn by the girls, and to observe the embroidered jackets of the men. And we not only see these worn, but also see them in the making. Many of the women, as they stand behind their stalls waiting for customers, deftly apply the needle to jackets, bodices, aprons, and caps, which are offered for sale. Quimper is known as a "religious" town, and there are usually large groups of people in the churches. The "Pardon" here usually takes place the last Sunday in July, when all routes to the city have temporary shrines, sometimes garlanded with the branches of trees and containing images of saints that have been brought from distant villages.

The Cathedral, a work of three centuries, is usually called the finest Gothic church in Brittany. The west portal dates from 1425 and has an openwork balustrade decorated with sculpture. Between the towers is an equestrian statue of King Grallon. Inside are the fifteenth-century nave, the ten Flamboyant windows, and the pulpit, which has decorations showing St. Carentin's fish. This fish, we are told, provided the saint's daily meal, yet always reappeared in the pool near

HARBOR OF QUIMPER WITH THE CATHEDRAL IN THE BACKGROUND

LOOKING UP THE MAIN STREET OF QUIMPER TOWARD THE CATHEDRAL

A TYPICAL STREET IN QUAINT OLD QUIMPER

his cell. In the streets we may study Breton life, the life of the unassuming, affable people for whom this part of France is noted. What a pleasure it is to wander through the streets, to see the old houses, to mingle with the picturesque characters whom we find in the market-place and crowding the thoroughfares! No better example of the old-fashioned but good-natured Breton woman could

BELLES OF PONT L'ABBE

be found, than a kindly old lady seated in the market-place; she is eagerly trying to dispose of her wares, but, fearful lest she lose a moment's time, when no purchaser is near she keeps busy crocheting or mending.

From Quimper we motor to Pont l'Abbé, the capital of the Bigouden, a race differing in many respects from the other Bretons and supposed to be descendants of a pre-Celtic population. Here we see some of the finest costumes in Brittany, many of them elaborately embroidered. Some of the Pont l'Abbé girls are beautiful with their large dark eyes and hair as black as a raven. They understand the art of adornment and are as particular about their attire as any girl in a metropolitan city. Most of them are experts with the needle, and, with full knowledge of their charms, add largely to their incomes by posing for artists or by exacting substantial fees from photographers. They are shrewd enough to know that they can get a round price from the enthusiastic

man with a camera. Pont l'Abbé is the chief town of the
Bigouden, which takes its name from the unusual headdress
of the women. This consists of a high conical lace coif and a
small bonnet. The women also wear black bodices and the
men black jackets, both embroidered with arabesques of
yellow.

A few miles from here is the Penmarch lighthouse, one of
the largest in the world. At one time Penmarch was a flour-

MENDING HIS NETS AT CONCARNEAU

ishing city, but the discovery of the Grand Banks of New-
foundland and the disappearance of the codfish ruined the
town in the sixteenth century. All that is likely to interest
us about the place is the curious church of the sixteenth century, which has a round arch portal of 1508 and a pretty
window with a fleur-de-lys tracery. Its only inhabitants now
are fisher-folk, who manage somehow to eke out an existence.
Their bronzed faces, Breton beards, and curly hair are attrac-

tions which bring them a partial living by posing for artists, and the balance comes from the sale of fish.

Another fishing village, but much larger and more important, is Concarneau, the center of the sardine fishery. Nowhere are the costumes more unusual, and if one is fortunate enough to be here at the time of a "Pardon" it is a sight worth while. The men are as interesting as the women, and take as much pains to wear becoming attire. The fête is attended by peasants from far and near, and is a scene of great rejoicing and holiday-making. Concarneau is a magnet for American art students.

The waitress at our hotel at Pont Aven, a charming maid, told us of a wedding to take place in the suburbs, and as she was an invited guest, took upon herself the responsibility of including us as guests of the wedding. Arriving on the scene,

FISHING FLEET IN THE HARBOR OF CONCARNEAU

[117]

WOMEN OF PONT AVEN IN THEIR SUNDAY BEST

we found the wedding party having a jolly time, dancing in the road and preparing for the feast which was to follow. A present of a gold coin removed all the shyness of the bridal couple, and they consented to pose for us, arrayed in all their finery. Nothing was lacking but the minister who was to officiate at the ceremony, but who had evidently overslept, and the guests were anxiously awaiting his arrival. As we rode back to town, we passed a row of children perched on a wall, and we could not resist the temptation to take with us the pretty picture, wooden shoes and all.

We stop in Quimperlé only long enough to take a hurried glimpse of the town and busy streets. There is little to keep us here for more than a few hours.

Arriving at Hennebont, we find the streets crowded with peasants. The market-place is a beehive of industry, as it is market-day, when everyone wants to buy or sell—the one day when Hennebont awakens and is full of life. The women wear large bonnets and a curious costume seen only here. Historically, Hennebont is unrivaled in interest, and it is the most strongly fortified town in Brittany. It was captured after a bloodless battle by the Earl of Montfort, who convinced the inhabitants of his right to govern. Later the Earl was made a prisoner, and the castle was

BEAUX OF PONT AVEN

besieged by the French, who were defeated through the bravery of a woman known to the Bretons as Jeanne la Flamme. To this day the Bretons believe that the ghost of this brave woman haunts the castle.

One of the strangest parts of the Morbihan is the narrow tongue of land stretching into the ocean, the Peninsula of Quiberon. It is so narrow that at one place there is room only for the road and the railway track. The Bay of Quiberon is a

PICTURESQUE OLD QUIMPERLE

place of terrible memories. It was here that the great naval fight took place between Cæsar's fleet and the two hundred and twenty ships of the Veneti, the people who inhabited this portion of Brittany at the time of the coming of the Romans. It was a gallant defense that the barbarians, as Cæsar called them, put up when they found themselves face to face with the skilled legions of Rome. There is no knowing what the result might have been, had not the treacherous wind,

THE PRIDE OF HENNEBONT

which at first favored them, suddenly dropped, leaving their ships stranded. They had no oars, as the Romans had, so were helpless; and then followed the awful massacre of which the Romans have left record.

The Veneti are gone, but some other remarkable inhabitants are still here. From the bed of the ocean the fishermen bring to the surface huge spiny lobsters, or rather crawfish, struggling vainly to free themselves from the

GOTHIC GATEWAY AT HENNEBONT

meshes of the net in which they have entangled themselves. *Langoustes,* the French call them, and their flaky white meat is delicious. Monster crabs are also denizens of the deep in Morbihan Bay. One must know how to handle such crustaceans, else they may sink their claws into one's flesh, refusing to let go. They have been known to permit their claws to be broken rather than let loose their hold.

Retracing our steps across the Quiberon Peninsula, we visit Carnac, the center of the mysterious Druidical region. As far as the eye can see, eleven rows of stone menhirs stretch away; an army of motionless phantoms they appear, as we view them from a height. There are in all about eighteen hundred stones still standing; originally there were between twelve and fifteen thousand. Some of them are as much as sixteen feet in height and weigh from forty to sixty tons. Their history is a sealed book; but they no doubt

MARKET DAY AT HENNEBONT, ON THE COAST OF BRITTANY

mark a burial place of the Druids. Remarkable examples of these megalithic monuments may be found at Locmariaquer. Here we still find the original vaults undisturbed; even the sacrificial stones may be distinguished. Huge boulders forming Druid graves are numerous in this vicinity. On some of them is still to be seen curious carving not unlike that found in the temples of Egypt.

"LANGOUSTES," MONSTER LOBSTERS OF
THE CHANNEL WATERS

The Grand Menhir is of such gigantic proportions that one wonders whence it came and how they got it to this place. Were it possible to tear the veil of mystery from these ancient graves, a new history might be revealed to us, a story of an almost unknown people, who were here long before Rome conquered the world.

Men and boys in Locmariaquer wear quaint and picturesque Breton hats, with streamers of ribbons. This town is known as "the place of the Virgin Mary," and here are several stone monuments of great interest to students. At the right, as we enter the village, we see a round barrow with a dolmen, which is known locally as "the hill of ashes." A path leads from here to the largest menhir in the world, which towers to a height of seventy-six feet. It is of granite, foreign to the neighborhood, and is estimated to weigh over three hundred tons. It has several companions, one of which is enclosed by a wall.

These stones are said to be monuments marking graves that were dug after a great battle, now forgotten. It has been argued by other archeologists that they may have been set up to protect Roman camps. Local tradition has it that each one of the monuments is an ancient warrior turned to stone. Historians have asserted that the stones were arranged

TWO THOUSAND OF THESE GREAT "MENHIRS" STILL STAND
IN THE "ALINEMENTS" AT CARNAC

[123]

BRETON PEASANTS IN THEIR SUNDAY ATTIRE

so as to indicate the direction of the sunrise at the solstices and the equinox, thus fixing the time of the rites of an ancient sun-worship. We know comparatively little of the religion of the Druids; in fact, one of their laws was, "Do not discuss religion among yourselves," and it has been called the "gray cult," because it was doubtless a mystery to most of the believers in it. Other laws were: "Women may be judges and arbiters"; "usury is theft, and you owe the usurer nothing"; "foreign merchants are forbidden to import luxuries among us"; "marry your wife without a dowry"; and, "no child shall be brought up in the cities—the children shall be brought up in the villages, otherwise the republic has no use for them." Julius Cæsar wrote: "It is a law of the Druids that no man shall be richer than his neighbor."

The "Pardon" of St. Cornély occurs at Carnac in September. St. Cornély is popular because it was he who turned the Roman soldiers to stone when they sought to enter the city. Do they not stand there to-day as proof of his miracle? And this saint also protects horned cattle. On the day of his fête, the cattle, wearing ribbons, flowers, and rosettes, are brought to the door of the church, where they are blessed by the clergy and sprinkled with holy water. The presence of one of these animals in a whole herd will protect the others from disease.

Center of the sardine fishing industry, Concarneau is also a place where artists go. Its harbor filled with boats and sails of many colors affords a beautiful sight for tourist and artist alike. The original town is enclosed within the walls of an ancient fortification. A new city has risen outside the old walls—a city which has become both a resort and a center of fishing industry as well. In huge tanks, tens of thousands of crabs and lobsters are cached for Paris epicures.

Brest, a city of something over seventy thousand inhabitants, is of interest to the visitor chiefly as a center for excursions in Finistere, the "Land's End" of Brittany. It made progress as a commercial port during the last war, as it was a base of the American army in France. It is usually called the rainiest of all French cities. The city is mentioned in chronicles as early as the ninth century; but the dockyard owes its creation to Richelieu. There is a busy water scene here, and several pleasant excursions by boat may be of interest; but travelers from America usually prefer to pass along to prettier places after they have glanced at the principal sights.

Across the Bay of Douarnenez, we come to Audierne, where we are likely to hear many familiar legends, none perhaps so well known as that of Ys, which forms the basis of Lalo's

SOME ARE ENGAGED COUPLES AND DON'T CARE WHO KNOWS IT

CHILDREN OF BRITTANY IN THEIR SUNDAY BEST

familiar opera, "Le Roi d'Ys." It appears that Ys was a very wicked city, and the wickedest person there was the Princess Dahut, daughter of the King. As in the legend of Tamara, there was an awful abyss over which she flung her discarded lovers. God wished to punish the inhabitants for their wickedness. The dikes and locks of the city could be opened only by a golden key, which the King wore suspended from his neck. His daughter stole it while he slept, and wickedly unlocked the water gates. The waters rushed in to submerge the city, and the King was warned to flee. He started to take the princess with him, but the voice of God warned him to leave her behind. After he had obeyed, the flood subsided somewhat, but the city remained submerged, and the next day only the waters of the bay could be seen where the city had stood. And now the fishermen say that on stormy days

[127]

they have seen church spires in the trough of the waves, and have heard the bells ringing the hymn of the day. The subject has also served as the inspiration of a well-known composition by Debussy.

We are not likely to go there, but it is worth knowing that a short side-trip from Quimper will bring us to La Faouet, a quaint and primitive town, the patron saint of which is St. Fiacre, the protector of horticulture and of Paris cabmen. We are told that an Irishman took to Paris several plants hitherto unknown, which gave an impetus to horticulture. He chose St. Fiacre for his patron and prospered, so a friend who inaugurated a line of public carriages had the saint's portrait painted on every vehicle. Thus did this particular saint give his name to the well-known "fiacre" of the capital. Near La Faouet are the remains of a château and one of the most interesting archeological objects in the province, called "The Venus of Quinipily," which stands six feet high. The origin of the statue is unknown; some say it is Egyptian, others think it is Roman work. Prosper Merimée was inclined to believe that it belonged to the sixteenth century, but modern specialists believe it to be much older. It has certain characteristics of Isis and may have accompanied Oriental legions that were in the Roman army and that brought along their goddess for protection. Locally it is called "The Sorceress of the Guard," a name that dates from ancient times; and it has been venerated by the inhabitants for several centuries, being specially invoked by men and women who desire children. The clergy objected to this and threw the stone in the river, where it remained for a long time; but the people finally rescued it. The count who owned the château at the time placed it upon a pedestal, and the cult was revived.

VII   ON THE WAY TO NANTES

GERTRUDE VANDERBILT WHITNEY MONUMENT AT ST. NAZAIRE

VII

ON THE WAY TO NANTES

FROM Quiberon let us go on a pleasant excursion by steamer to Belle-Ile, the most important of the Breton islands, which is little more than a plateau of slate, but shows in certain places a tropical vegetation that is surprising. Belle-Ile is said to have sixty safe harbors, and there is a romantic interest in the fact that the island was ceded by the Abbés of St. Croix to Marshal de Retz (or Rais), who was the original of all the Breton Blue Beard legends. Dumas has placed a scene from this island in "The Three Musketeers," and Balzac made it the scene of one of his novels. Perhaps the most recent celebrity to become associated with the place was Sarah Bernhardt, the actress, who liked to spend her summer holidays in one of the towers of the deserted fortifications. A tour of the whole island may be accomplished in a single day.

We may then go to Vannes, a modern town with a splendid city hall, a large square, and numerous substantial streets. This will be almost our last opportunity to see people in peculiar costumes. We go direct to the Cathedral, which was rebuilt in the thirteenth century. The nave has lost its ancient appearance and character, but there are interesting tombs in the aisle chapels. Paintings illustrating the life of St. Vincent Ferrer, the tomb of the saint, and badly worn tapestries depicting his miracles and canonization are worth seeing. In the old Parliament House is now installed the

Archeological Museum, which contains some exceedingly rare prehistoric items, chiefly taken from the barrows and stone monuments of the neighborhood.

St. Nazaire is a port city that will be remembered by many of the American doughboys, who first touched the European Continent here when they joined the soldiers of the Allies in 1917-18. It is an industrial and marine center of considerable importance (it is the seventh seaport in France), but the visitor is unlikely to find much here that interests him, and after a glance he will probably leave for the more unusual and picturesque localities. Through the generosity of Gertrude Vanderbilt Whitney, a memorial has been erected in St. Nazaire representing an American youth, sword in hand, riding on the back of an American eagle. He seems to be saying to the people of France: "You sent for me; here I am!"

From the estuary of the Loire we travel toward Nantes

WOMEN TAKING THEIR PRODUCE TO MARKET AT VANNES

by a roundabout route that will enable us to visit several interesting towns of the interior.

Rennes, a city with about eighty thousand inhabitants, was the old capital of Brittany and is now important as a railway center, which recalls the fact that in Roman times it had a similar distinction as the center of a network of highways. In 1720, the place was visited by a fire that swept through the streets for seven days, resulting in the destruction of many of the old buildings; these were re-

BOYS OF ST. NAZAIRE

placed by formal structures of red granite, so that the town lacks the picturesque appearance of some of its neighbors. A generation ago Rennes was a center of world interest as the scene of the celebrated Dreyfus trial.

We visit the former university building, which contains several very good collections: antiquities, a Breton museum, and a picture gallery. The Breton items consist chiefly of costumes and furniture. The Palais de Justice, an important building, was erected in the seventeenth century, and preserves the style of the Renaissance period. The corner pavilions are surmounted by lead allegorical figures, and the entrance has statues of distinguished members of the bar of Rennes. The former seminary is now the home of the Faculté des Lettres and of the Library; the latter contains several

THE SOLID CITIZENS OF A PROSPEROUS BRETON COMMUNITY

important illuminated manuscripts: a "Roman de la Rose" and Holy Grail and Golden Legend versions.

The Cathedral has two towers, said to have been begun by Anne of Brittany, and the side entrances date from the Renaissance. We are interested in the interior of the church chiefly for a reredos, which shows splendid wood-carving of the fifteenth century and is notable for the number of its figures, among which we note the violin and bagpipe players in the stable at Bethlehem.

Next we visit Vitré, an ancient town in which there are several fine old buildings and picturesque timbered houses with carved pillars and quaint gables. The Castle, which dates from the eleventh century, is a good example of Breton military architecture. A pleasant drive of four miles out from the town brings us to the principal reason for visiting Vitré, namely, the Château des Rochers, famous as the residence of Madame de Sévigné, who dated nearly three hundred of her letters from the château or from Vitré. Visitors are admitted to the chapel, and to Madame's private room, known as the Cabinet Vert, which contains her bed with a coverlet embroidered by her daughter, a toilet table, autographs, a bureau, and her portrait by Mignard; also to the French garden laid out by Le Notre, with a sun-dial and a wall that returns a double echo.

Madame's trips to Paris, so well described in her numerous letters, took eight or nine days. "It was a veritable cavalcade," she wrote; "two open carriages, seven carriage horses, two men on horseback, and upon a pack-horse the bed is carried to serve at the inns en route." There was always a welcome for Madame de Sévigné at Versailles, when Louis XIV was King. She wrote excellent travel letters, of which a critic has said: "The most interesting thing in them is herself."

It is fascinating to think of her going up to Paris and making a reentry into the society of Racine, Voltaire, Corneille, La Fontaine and Molière; but it is even more interesting to follow her in her daily life at Les Rochers, reading, planting avenues of trees, and going to Vitré to attend the assembling of the Breton parliament. On these latter occasions, she tells us, "the dinners are so magnificent that one dies of hunger," adding, as she goes back to her château: "I need to sleep, to eat, to refresh myself, to be silent." From Les Rochers she writes: "We rise at eight. I often spend the hour until nine in the park, breathing the fresh air of the forest. At nine, the bell rings for mass. After mass, we make our toilette and say good morning to one another. We gather flowers; we dine. Between dinner and five we read and write. When I go to my apartment, I have my books. I plant myself

CLEANING THE DAY'S CATCH

wherever I like. I change places and I change books—for one a book of devotion, for another history, and so on. At eight I hear a bell. It is for supper. After which we sit in the garden listening to the nightingales and breathing the perfume of the orange blossoms." Madame was a most unusual person, enjoying whatever life offered, from the books of Rabelais to "The Lives of the Saints," from the altar of

BRETON BELLES IN GALA COSTUME

the chapel at Les Rochers to a dance at Versailles as the partner of Louis XIV.

A short journey from Vitré brings us to Châteaubriant, an old town of about seven thousand inhabitants. The place derives its name from a stronghold founded in the eleventh century. Both the new and the old portions of the château are worth visiting. It is but a two-hour railway journey from here to Nantes.

Nantes, now an important industrial city, is at the junction of the Loire and Erdre, the former being navigable by

large vessels from the sea, which lies thirty miles distant.
The islands formed by many river branches are linked by
eighteen bridges. Away back in the Gaelic period, Nantes
was a place of importance, as it was during the Roman occupation. It was Christianized as early as the third century
by St. Clair, and in the fifth century it was the seat of government of a Breton chieftain. There are several historical
characters with whom we should become acquainted at
Nantes, as there are souvenirs of them in this city, and a
recollection of their lives enhances our interest. Anne of
Brittany was born here. John Knox was kept prisoner here
as a galley slave. In the last war, the city was a temporary
British base and later a supply station for the American
army.

First of all, we go to the Castle, now public property,

RUBBER BOOTS ARE BETTER THAN BARE TOES IN A LOBSTER CACHE

EVEN THE BABIES ARE OUT TO SEE HOW THE MOVIE CAMERA WORKS

which dates its foundation from the tenth century. It was the residence of Duke Francis II, father of Anne; and one of the towers is pointed out as the prison of Gilles de Retz, the Marshal of France, who is credited with the murder of over one hundred children, sacrificed to devil-worship. He was hanged and burned at Nantes, the scene of his crimes. The house from which the celebrated Edict of Nantes was issued in 1598 is still existent.

The Cathedral, which dates from the fifteenth century, is not impressive from the exterior, but we go inside to see the marble tomb of Francis II and his second wife, considered a masterpiece of French Renaissance sculpture. This tomb was erected—in the first years of the sixteenth century—for Anne of Brittany, probably the most celebrated of all Breton women, as she was twice Queen of France. Anne's heart

AN OUTDOOR LAUNDRY IN BRITTANY

ALL A LITTLE SELF-CONSCIOUS UNDER A NEW EXPERIENCE

once reposed in this tomb. The effigies of the Duke and Duchess rest upon a black marble slab, with a lion and grayhound at their feet, and guarded by figures of Justice, Strength, Moderation and Prudence. In the upper niches are apostles and saints, and mourners in the lower spaces. Anne's body lies at St. Denis, in Paris, by the resting-place of her husbands, Charles VIII and Louis XII; but she requested that her heart, ever

AT THE PUBLIC WELL

loyal to Brittany, might be sent to Nantes after her death.

Anne's mother died when she was young, but the daughter shared the confidence of her father and usually accompanied him upon his expeditions. After the death of her father (when she was fourteen years of age) her duchy was threatened, but she was the richest heiress in Europe, and any prince to whom she could bring Brittany as a dower would hold the balance of power.

The Prince of Orange sought her hand, but she declared publicly that she detested him. When she heard of a plan to kidnap her and force her submission, she galloped off on horseback, accompanied by a suite, and asked Nantes to receive her. The ambassador of the Prince reached the city before her, and an effort was made to capture her, instead of offering her asylum in her hour of need. Again she galloped away, and after spending two weeks in the fields, she said she would enter a cloister if forced to marry the Prince. Called

[141]

to Rennes by faithful subjects, she made a grand entrance into that town and took the oath of office before parliament. Charles VIII of France was deficient in mind and body, but when he asked Anne to marry him, she could see no other way out of her difficulties and consented. She loved the King's cousin, a pretender, the Duke of Orleans, and he loved her; but sometimes kings have their way, and about two weeks after receiving the proposal of marriage, Anne rode off to Langeais on the Loire for the wedding ceremony. Says an old chronicle: "The Duchess Anne came to the castle attended by a great train of Breton lords and ladies, and she brought rich store of clothing and of household plenishing. Most magnificent of all her robes was her wedding gown of cloth of gold of more than ten thousand pounds in value, and its train and her mantle were bordered with an hundred

AN IVY-CLAD COTTAGE IN WESTERN FRANCE

and sixty skins of ermine."

Anne prospered famously as Queen, being able and tactful. When she heard that Orleans had offered an expression of regard for her, she had him banished. But six years after the marriage, Charles died and his widow returned to Brittany. After four months of widowhood, the lady, then only twenty-one years of age, married Louis XII and again mounted the throne of France. There was a marked change in her man-

TOO BUSY TO LOOK UP

ner, and it was observed that she had become a genuine sovereign and diplomat. The King treated her with respect, and she had her own bodyguard—mostly of Bretons. At the age of thirty-seven she died, and while the Parisians lighted four thousand candles for her funeral at Notre Dame, the Bretons, not to be outdone, lighted five thousand candles when her heart was received at Nantes.

This may not be what the visitor would consider a town of "sights," but it is a delightful old place of fragrant memories, and one who has the leisure will like to remain for several days. There are many worth-while excursions to be made. For example, the trip on the Loire from Nantes to St. Nazaire and back. The steamers run daily; the water trip takes less than four hours, and the boat steams along through a beautiful country. Or the trip to Lège, taking one through St. Philibert-de-Grand-Lieu, which has an an-

SWEETHEARTS

cient church that preserves several features of the Carlovingian period — almost the only example in France. The crypt contains the ninth-century tomb of St. Philibert, founder of the famous Abbey of Jumièges in Normandy.

It takes only about one hour to reach Clisson from Nantes, and anyone who loves romantic associations will not fail to make this sentimental journey. Not far from the castle at Clisson is Le Palet, a small village, where Abelard was born. It was in a grotto here that he and Heloise sought solitude in the early period of their troubles. Here their child was born, and from here they went to Paris, where—at Père la Chaise—their graves are seen by ardent lovers, who still think with pity of the unhappy pair of the eleventh century. In a lonely spot on the shore of the gulf, we come upon the ruins of the Abbey of St. Gildas, where Abelard passed years of torment, persecuted by the monks.

An hour on the railway takes us from Clisson to Tiffauges, where is situated what usually is considered the most important of the Blue Beard castles, of which there are so many. We have noted how Gilles de Retz, Marshal of France, met his deserved death at Nantes; here was the scene of his chief revels. Under Charles VII, he was one of the bravest generals of France. He became very powerful, and was the lord of many castles, some of which were luxuriously furnished. At Tiffauges he supported a company of two hundred knights, a large troupe of comedians, a chapel with thirty monks, a boy choir, many instrumentalists, and a numerous retinue of servants, who were costumed like the servants of princes. When he went beyond his castle, he was accompanied by this spectacular retinue, which gave him the appearance of an Oriental potentate. His chapel was enriched with ornaments of gold, and he had an organ that was carried with him everywhere. Then, when he had squandered much of his fortune, he plunged into the study of alchemy and sorcery. In the castle at Tiffauges, the assassinations took place, and the Black Mass was celebrated in the chapel. With his own hands, tradition says, he strangled children in the midst of his orgies, and led infamous ceremonial proces-

THE OLDER PEASANT WOMEN REFUSE TO FOLLOW THE DICTATES OF FASHION

[145]

sions, followed by his chaplains and servants. He specialized in refined cruelties. The inhabitants of the region believed that their children were carried off by fairies, whereas they were collected by his agents as they were tending their flocks in the fields. Finally, the secrets were told by his servants and the matter was brought to the attention of the Bishop of Nantes; and when threatened with torture, he confessed to enough crimes to hang a dozen men.

PEASANT GIRLS, ONE IN WOODEN SHOES

VIII THE BEAUTIFUL CHATEAUX

CHATEAU USSE HAS A DELIGHTFULLY PICTURESQUE SETTING

VIII

THE BEAUTIFUL CHATEAUX

MANY of the most important events in French history, during the period from Charles VII to Henry IV, transpired along the banks of the Loire; and some of the most interesting edifices of the country are here, all associated with the lives of celebrated persons, who left their names written large in the national chronicles.

We arrive at Angers, where we see the first of the Loire châteaux and also the fine old city that was once the capital of the duchy of Anjou. It was a place of importance in Gallic and Roman times and has figured prominently in many wars. The Cathedral dates from the twelfth and thirteenth centuries and is a fine example of Gothic architecture. The main portal has four statues of Biblical personages on each side, and in the tympanum is the figure of Jesus surrounded by symbols of the Evangelists. The central tower, which dates from the sixteenth century, has a cupola and lantern with eight statues representing St. Maurice and his associates in the full military costumes of the sixteenth century. The interior of the church has many things to please the eye, and during the summer months several splendid tapestries are displayed, the finest of the collection being one three hundred feet long, representing the Apocalypse, which was presented by King René.

On the second floor of the museum is a good collection of pictures, among some of the best being: "Portrait," by Ribera; "Venice," by Ziem; "The Refuge of Innocence," by Vigée Le Brun; "Two Portraits of Children," by Henner; "Greek Tragedians," by Ingres; a ceiling design by Tiepolo, a restored "Holy Family" by Raphael, a landscape by Ruysdael; "Madame de Porcin," by Greuze, and "Mary of Magdala," by Puvis de Chavannes.

The Castle at Angers is one of the best-preserved feudal structures in France. It dates from the thirteenth century. It is an irregular pentagon in shape, and has seventeen large towers, with a moat one hundred feet wide and thirty-six feet deep—all hewn out of the solid rock. The interior of this pile is likely to provide only slight interest; but one is advised to walk around the ramparts, which provide an excel-

CASTLE OF ANGERS: A POWERFUL FEUDAL STRONGHOLD

lent view. An adjoining pavilion is said to have been the
birthplace of King René.

Saumur is a fine old town, with a population of about
sixteen thousand, situated on land between the Loire and the
Thouet, and is completely dominated by its Castle, an impressive structure with four angle towers. It probably dates
from the tenth century. It was acquired by the municipality

SAUMUR HAS A MEDIEVAL CASTLE CONTAINING
A MUSEUM OF ANTIQUITIES

in 1906 and now houses the museum. There are paintings
and antiquities on the lower floors, and the third is devoted
to the Museum of the Horse, containing a good collection of
harness, bits, and stirrups.

Langeais is known chiefly on account of its Castle, the
ruins of which may be among the oldest in France. The
present building, a fine example of the feudal stronghold,

SAUMUR, ON THE LOIRE, ONE OF THE EARLY CENTERS OF
PROTESTANTISM IN FRANCE

dates from the fifteenth century. In 1491, the marriage of
Charles VII and Anne of Brittany was celebrated here. We
approach it by a flight of steps from the town, and the draw-
bridge is defended by three large towers with conical roofs.
The room in which the famous marriage took place, has tapestries, chests, and beds of the fifteenth and sixteenth centuries. From the third floor we make a tour of the covered
rampart walk and obtain excellent views of the town and
the valley. Opposite the castle is a house of the Renaissance
period, in which, we are told, Rabelais was once a visitor.

Near Chinon we pass some curious cave-houses in the side
of a mountain. They are hewn out of the solid rock and
contain various chambers. Some of them are quite artistic
and have the appearance of being occupied by people in comfortable circumstances. They are embellished and orna-

mented like substantial residences and are no doubt cool in the summer and warm in winter. It is strange to see several miles of these houses, where the people, like moles, have burrowed deep into the hill.

The Castle of Chinon consists of three strongholds separated by deep moats. The Château du Milieu is the largest, and is on the site of a Roman structure. Overlooking the town is the palace where Henry II died and where Charles VII received Jeanne d'Arc in 1429. On the left and approached by a bridge is the Château du Coudray, in which the Maid of Orleans remained in care of the governor.

The Château of Azay-le-Rideau is justly held to be among the most beautiful products of the Renaissance. It has been called a diamond in an emerald setting. This very attractive mansion, washed on three sides by the river, was purchased

CHATEAU OF LANGEAIS AND ITS PECULIAR GARDEN

[153]

CAVE HOUSE AT CHINON

by the state in 1905 and now contains a museum of Renaissance tapestry, bronze, furniture, and carvings. The ceiling of the staircase is decorated with medallions of the Kings of France.

The center of the château district is Tours, a delightful old city, situated between the Loire and the Cher, and much favored by foreigners on account of its natural charm and excellent climate. The limits of the old town are well defined by the tree-bordered boulevards that follow the line of the ancient ramparts. Even the town itself is divided, the Cathedral quarter being on the site of old Tours and the west quarter occupying the site of Châteauneuf, now the most interesting part of the city to the visitor. Tours is the most convenient center for a tour of the château country, and an excellent motor service has been provided for short excursions.

Tours has had a notable history. It was the Gallic Altionos, and later, when it moved across the river, it became the Cæsarodunum of the Romans. The present name appears in the fourth century, and it is believed that Christianity was flourishing here as early as the third century. St. Martin, the great apostle of France, was Bishop of Tours, and Honoré de Balzac, the great novelist, was born here. It was a chief supply base of the American army during the Great War.

First of all, we make our way to the Cathedral, a fine

edifice, despite its rather modest dimensions when compared to some of the great churches of France. The church was in the process of construction from 1220 to 1547; thus it is a good example of every type of French Gothic construction. There are three Flamboyant entrances, and the central window has two towers, while the façades have splendid rose windows that date from the fourteenth century. The interior is notable for its stained glass windows. The tombs of the sons of Charles VII are in the first choir chapel. The Lady Chapel has frescoes, and it is worth while to climb to the top of the south tower, whence an excellent view is obtained. Behind the Cathedral, in a gable of the old archbishop's chapel, is an open-air pulpit.

The Musée des Beaux-Arts occupies the old archbishop's palace, which dates from the seventeenth and eighteenth

CHINON, WITH ITS TRIPLE CHATEAU, HAS A MEDIEVAL AIR

[155]

AZAY-LE-RIDEAU, ONE OF THE MOST PLEASING OF THE
RENAISSANCE CHATEAUX

centuries, with parts of an earlier building, built onto the
ancient Gallo-Roman town wall. There are several paintings here that we should see, including: Mantegna's "Resur-
rection" and "Christ in the Garden," two pictures which,
with the "Christ between the Thieves" (now in the Louvre
at Paris), made an altar-piece in San Zeno at Verona;
Rubens's "Mars Crowned by Victory"; Legros's "Artist's
Father," and several other pictures of value. On the first
floor are Tours silk, Sèvres porcelain, enamels and pottery.
On the second floor are modern paintings and engravings.
The Museum of Touraine Antiquities contains a notable collection of Roman, Gallo-Roman, Merovingian, and other
antiquities. The Library has over one hundred thousand
volumes, a collection of two thousand manuscripts, including a prayer-book of Charles V, an eleventh-century "Life

of St. Martin," and early editions of the classics. The Church of St. Julien belonged to an abbey founded in the fifth century. The site of the ancient Basilica of St. Martin has fragments of the splendid church over the tomb of the saint. Here was the great center of the pilgrimage which his tomb attracted, and excavations in the last century resulted in the finding of the tomb again. The New Basilica of St. Martin has a large dome surmounted by a statue of the saint. The nave columns are monoliths of Vosges granite, and the saint's tomb is beneath the choir.

The first important château that we encounter in ascending the Loire from Tours is Amboise. Overlooking the river from the high left bank, the massive structure looks more like a fortified castle than a Renaissance palace. Many historic events have taken place within its walls, for it belonged

THE HANDSOME CATHEDRAL OF TOURS IS JOSTLED BY BUSINESS

to one branch or another of the royal family for centuries. A great tragedy visited it during the religious wars, and the guide will point out to you the spot where 1200 Huguenots were murdered in 1560 when they conspired to remove by force the young King Francis II from the influence of the Guises. Three years later the Edict of Amboise granted toleration to the Huguenots. Out in the great courtyard, in the massive Chapel of St. Hubert, is the tomb of the great

THE HOTEL DE VILLE AT TOURS

Italian artist, Leonardo da Vinci, who was engaged in work here for Francis I when he died in 1519.

Charmingly situated on a wooded ridge is the Château of Chaumont. It is a mixture of late Gothic and Renaissance, and has the appearance of a feudal castle. Built by Cardinal d'Amboise, it was purchased in 1560 by Catherine de Medici. Frequently restored, it is modern in appearance.

Of all the châteaux in Touraine, none excels in historic signficance the Château of Blois. Louis XII was born here;

within its walls Anne of Brittany and Catherine de Medici died. It has been for ages the residence of Kings and Queens, and the last imperial decree of Napoleon I was dated here. Blois, now a town of about thirty thousand inhabitants, has picturesque, narrow streets and many interesting buildings, being a pleasant central place in which to remain while visiting near-by châteaux. The place was important, even in Roman times, and it passed to the crown of France when

CHAPEL AT AMBOISE

Louis XII succeeded to the throne. Here Louis XIII imprisoned his mother, Marie de Medici, for two years. In the eighteenth century the castle became a barrack, but it has been restored and should be visited. The exterior is usually counted a masterpiece of the Renaissance period in one wing and a fine example of the classic in another. On the first floor are the Library and the Salle des Fêtes, which latter has some fine Gobelin tapestries. On this floor are also the Queen's apartments, once occupied by Catherine de Medici. On the second floor are the apartments of Henri III, to which we mount by the famous Escalier des Quarante-Cinq, named for the forty-five servants who assisted in the murder of the Duke of Guise and his brother, Cardinal de Guise. There are fine fireplaces in the council chamber, and in the so-called Galérie d'Honneur du Roi, which has five rooms, we visit the oratory where Henri posted two monks to pray "for the success of a great undertaking" while the murder was being committed. The State Chamber is a large hall, the vaulted roof of which is ornamented with fleurs-de-lis. The Musée has some interesting paintings, mostly by French artists, altho there are a few good primitives.

We may also visit the Cathedral of Blois, the tower of which has a twelfth-century foundation. Behind the church are the Art Museum and a museum of archeology and natural history. In the adjoining park is a statue of Jeanne d'Arc.

There are many delightful excursions into the environs of Blois. One of about twenty-five miles takes us to Château-renault, to reach which we pass through the beautiful oak forest of Blois and come upon the Church of Coulanges, which has stalls from the twelfth-century Abbey La Guiche;

CHATEAU OF AMBOISE SEEN ACROSS THE LOIRE

BATTLEMENTED TOWERS OF THE CHATEAU OF CHAUMONT

also upon the ruined Château de Bury, and Herbault with its eighteenth-century château.

Situated in a park twenty miles square, the Château of Chambord, one of the finest palaces of the Renaissance, attracts many visitors. Built for Francis I, it has been enlarged several times. Louis XV made many changes in the original building, and Marshal Saxe, to whom it was presented, made further alterations. Stanislaus Lesczinski, ex-King of Poland, lived in it for eight years. Finally Napoleon presented it to one of his Marshals. Within is a double spiral staircase, where one person may ascend and another descend at the same time and one cannot see the other. It is a clever arrangement, but apparently without purpose. In one of the rooms are the playthings used by the Comte de Chambord when he was a boy. He was offered the throne of

GENERAL VIEW OF BLOIS AND ITS CATHEDRAL

BEAUTIFUL STAIRCASE IN THE CHATEAU OF BLOIS

France, but declined to accept it when the country refused to change the colors of the national flag to those of the Chambords. The sleeping-room of the Duke still contains the bed which he used. Tho he never reigned, a throne adorns the bed. Most of the rooms are now bare, the furniture having been removed.

ENTRANCE TO BLOIS CHATEAU

One of the most beautiful of all the châteaux is Chenonceaux. Spanning the river Cher, it has a unique situation. Surrounding it are magnificent gardens. It was here that Mary Queen of Scots and Francis II spent their honeymoon. Much of its beauty may be attributed to the liberality of Catherine de Medici, who expended considerable money in enlarging and embellishing it.

Another of the familiar châteaux is Usse, which, surrounded by gardens, dates from the fifteenth and sixteenth centuries. It has beautiful terraced gardens. We should not fail to have at least a glimpse of Villandry. Altho it is privately owned, the public is privileged to visit it on certain days and stroll around its sunken gardens, carpeted with flowers of many colors.

The trip to Romorantin provides a view of the fifteenth-century castle where Francis II signed an edict to prevent the establishment of the Inquisition in France. Another trip is to Vendôme, and still another to be recommended is that

CHAMBORD, ONE OF THE FINEST RENAISSANCE CHATEAUX

CHENONCEAUX, THE PALACE THAT SPANS A RIVER

to Montrichard, a quaint town with wooden houses that date from the fifteenth century.

If we have our own motor, we may go from here to Le Mans, a picturesque town of about seventy thousand inhabitants, which has much to interest us. This former Roman city was Christianized as early as the third century by St. Julian, and it has been the scene of many important events in French history. The Cathedral is usually counted

A MACHICOLATED TOWER
Handy for Dropping Molten Lead on Besiegers

as one of the most splendid in France, being dedicated to St. Julian and containing many items of interest. The tomb of Queen Berengaria, wife of Richard Cœur de Lion, is here; there is a fine rose window, the glass of which dates from the fifteenth century, and in the baptistery are notable tombs, like those of Charles d'Anjou and the Count of Maine. The treasury holds some excellent tapestries that at certain times are exhibited in the church.

The Eglise de la Couture has a beautiful porch of the thirteenth century, decorated with statues of the Apostles, and the tympanum has the "Last Judgment." The church is primitive Gothic, with no aisles, and the nave contains six noteworthy pictures by various artists, beginning on the right with "The Sleep of Elijah," by Philip de Champaigne, and ending with "St. Veronica," by Caracci. In the sacristy is preserved the shroud of St. Bernard. During the summer, several exquisite tapestries are exhibited on the walls of the church.

The Museum, which is installed in the former Benedictine Abbey of the Cultura, has paintings by Ary Scheffer, Corot, Ingres, Ribera, and Louis David, and a notable enameled copper portrait of the father of an English king. The last-named treasure is known as the "Enamel of Geoffrey Plantagenet," and is a placque two feet high bearing a likeness of Geoffrey, Count of Anjou, father of Henry II of England and founder of the Plantagenet line. The enameled portrait was intended for his tomb, but is now one of the sights of this museum in Le Mans.

IX   CHARTRES, ORLEANS, BOURGES

ONE OF FRANCE'S FINEST GOTHIC CATHEDRALS:
NOTRE DAME, AT CHARTRES

IX

CHARTRES, ORLEANS, BOURGES

EVERYONE who travels in France should go to the small city of Chartres for the purpose of seeing the Cathedral, one of the noblest examples of medieval architecture in the country. Chartres is a town of less than thirty thousand inhabitants. It has several features of interest; but it is the Cathedral that attracts our attention as we approach, and it is best to make our way to it soon after we have arrived. It is situated upon an elevation, above the red roofs of the town, and is the pivot around which the life of the place rotates. It was founded as early as the third century and occupies the site of a Druidical sanctuary devoted to the worship of a "Virgin destined to conceive." It was the earliest and the chief church of France dedicated to the Virgin Mary, and great pilgrimages were made to it centuries ago. The church was rebuilt and consecrated in its present form in the thirteenth century. Among its distinguishing features are: its immensity, the harmony of its design, the lateral portals, and its stained glass, especially its rose windows.

The Cathedral has a triple west portal of the twelfth century, ornamented with a hundred statues, chiefly illustrative of the life of Jesus. The central doorway has statues of royal saints, which show the Byzantine influence. A fine rose window is over this portal, formerly opened only for the King; and above the window is a gallery which contains sixteen statues of the Kings of Judah. The great north spire dates from 1514, and part of the expense was borne by Louis XII. There are two splendid side portals, still more elaborately decorated with large and small statues than the main entrance. Those of the north portal represent scenes from the life of the Virgin, and those of the south the Last Judgment.

The length of the church is four hundred twenty-two feet and its height slightly over one hundred feet. There are nearly two hundred stained-glass windows, much of the glass dating from the thirteenth century; the window showing the Tree of Jesse is still older. The choir has a splendid stone screen, decorated by forty statues representing events in the life of Jesus and the Virgin Mary. Behind the high altar are colossal figures depicting the Assumption. The

EVEN THE FLYING BUTTRESSES OF CHARTRES HAVE THEIR NICHES
AND STATUES

much venerated "Vièrge du
Pilier," dating from the
twelfth century, is in a
chapel north of the choir. It
was crowned with a "Lib-
erty" at the time of the Revolution.

The treasury contains a
celebrated "Garment of the
Virgin," which is said to have
been sent to Charlemagne by
the Empress Irene and presented to the church in the
ninth century. The crypt is
the largest in France and is
dedicated to the earliest of
the Christian Virgins on the site of the Druidical sanctuary.

SIDE VIEW SHOWING ONE OF THE
WHEEL WINDOWS

There are several monuments dedicated to local saints who
were bishops of Chartres.

It will be well, while we are here, to visit also St. Pierre's
Church, which contains some fine stained glass. There are
also twelve panels of Renaissance enamels, which were exe-
cuted for the castle chapel of Diane de Poitiers and represent
the twelve Apostles with their emblems. The Archeological
Museum has interesting pottery, sculptures, and Roman
antiquities found in the neighborhood. The Musée has
paintings by Claude Lorrain, Bouchot, Puvis de Chavannes,
tapestries, embroideries, and a collection of sixteenth-century
ivories.

From Chartres we go to one of the most alluring cities in
France, a place mellow with age and fragrant with the recollection of great events—Orleans, the most important city

THE SIDE PORTALS OF CHARTRES CATHEDRAL ARE MODELS OF
SCULPTURAL BEAUTY

between Paris and the Loire. We recall the words of Lave-
dan, who wrote: "Here all focuses itself into one great picture, the combined romance of an epoch. Have you not
been struck with a land where the clouds, the atmosphere,
the odor of the soil and the breezes from afar, all comport,
one with another, in true and just proportions?" This is
true of Orleans and its environs, a place that witnessed "the
morning of the Valois, the full noon of Louis XIV, and the
twilight of Louis XVI."

Orleans is a rare casket of jewels, each a souvenir of important events. Of special interest to all of us will be the reverence paid here to Jeanne d'Arc, her statue being placed in
many parts of the city, her picture displayed everywhere in
the shop-windows; and perhaps we shall be fortunate enough
to arrive here in the month of May, when the Maid's festival,

the most important event in the city's life, is being celebrated. Lemaître has written:

"I believe that the history of Jeanne d'Arc was the first that was ever told to me (before even the fairy tales of Perrault). The 'Mort de Jeanne d'Arc' of Casimir Delavigne was the first fable that I learned, and the equestrian statue of the 'Maid' in the Place Martroi, Orleans, is perhaps the oldest vision that my memory guards. This statue of Jeanne d'Arc is absurd. She has a Grecian profile, and a charger which is not a war-horse, but a race-horse. Nevertheless, to me it was noble and imposing. In the courtyard of the Hôtel de Ville is a *petite pucelle,* very gentle and pious, who holds against her heart her sword, after the manner of a crucifix. At the end of the bridge across the Loire is another Jeanne d'Arc, as the maid of war, surrounded by swirling draperies,

HOW ORLEANS HONORS THE "MAID OF ORLEANS," WHO RESCUED THE CITY FROM SIEGE

THE HOUSE AT ORLEANS IN WHICH JOAN OF ARC ONCE LIVED
(next to the hotel)

as in a picture of Juvenet's. This to me tells the whole story of the reverence with which the martyred 'Maid' is regarded in the city of Orleans by the Loire."

This city, however, does not contain so many monuments of past events as might be expected. The old town walls and gates have disappeared, and on their site are fine boulevards. It is the march of progress, and perhaps all are benefited thereby; still, the visitors who come for a few hours or days would prefer to see the city as it looked, say, on that celebrated spring day in 1429, when Jeanne d'Arc entered it and drove the English from their last stronghold. It was a blow from which the enemy never recovered, and the liberty of France was assured; an epoch-making event, which is celebrated here on May 8 each year, the standard of Jeanne being handed to the Bishop of Orleans the night before the fête, as he stands upon the illuminated steps of the Cathedral.

Orleans was an important city before the dawn of the Christian era, and doubtless was the Cenabum captured by Julius Cæsar in 52 B. C. As early as the third century, it was flourishing under the name of Aurelianum, from which its present name was derived. Clovis held here the first council called in France. During the religious wars, Condé made it the Protestant headquarters, and throughout the centuries it has continued to occupy a place of importance in national events.

The Cathedral was begun in 1601 by Henry IV, as a condition of his absolution by the Pope. Perhaps the most interesting feature of it is its good modern glass, representing the life of Jeanne d'Arc.

The Picture Gallery is in the buildings of the Hôtel des Créneaux and the old Hôtel de Ville, both dating from the early sixteenth century. The gallery is open to the public

ORLEANS CATHEDRAL, AN EXAMPLE OF LATE GOTHIC

on two days each week, and to visitors, upon application, at other times. Among its best possessions are: Rubens's "Genius and Triumph of the Arts," a portrait by Tintoretto, a landscape by Ruysdael, Teniers's "Gardener and Young Woman," Fragonard's "Offering to Cupid," Watteau's "The Ape a Sculptor," Houdon's "Rousseau and Voltaire" in terra-cotta, a "Madonna" by Correggio, and several important drawings by old masters.

The Musée Jeanne d'Arc contains relics and works of art associated with the heroine of the city. The ground floor has relics of the siege of 1429, and on the staircase are banners and escutcheons. On the first floor are tapestries, books relating to the siege, reproductions of statues, facsimiles of Jeanne's letters, autographs of distinguished contemporaries, statuettes, ivories, pottery and glass. The second floor has pewter, glass, pottery, seals, enamels, and many other items of local history. The third floor has paintings and sculptures referring to the "Maid." The Musée Fourche has a good collection of paintings, drawings, ivories, and other works of art. The paintings are chiefly of the French school, with examples of such masters from other lands as Raphael, Ribera, Rubens, Rembrandt and Jordaens. The Historical Museum occupies the former Hôtel Cabu. It has a notable collection of antiquities.

About ten miles distant is Cléry, famous for its Basilica of Notre Dame, a large church rebuilt by Louis XI in fulfil-ment of a vow made at the siege of Dieppe. We read in "Quentin Durward" of how the superstitious monarch, when held a captive by Charles the Bold, made his devotions to the little image, worn in his hat, of the Virgin of Cléry, "the grossness of his superstition, none the less than his fickleness, leading him to believe Our Lady of Cléry to be quite a dif-

IN THE JEANNE D'ARC MUSEUM AT ORLEANS

ferent person from the other object of his devotion, the Madonna of Embrun, a tiny mountain village in south-western France." Louis XI was buried in the church at Cléry, and his tomb attracts visitors, who also find here a stone that covers the heart of Charles VIII. Over the high altar is the miracle-working figure of Notre Dame de Cléry, a statue of oak that dates from the thirteenth century. Near the church is the "Maison de Louis XI," a house of brick, and in the Grande Rue is another building of the same name, now occupied by the Hôtel de la Belle Image, which appeals to sentimental visitors who like to live where royalty has dined and slept.

If we are interested in associations of places with celebrated people, we may go to Meung-sur-Loire, which has a statue of Jehan de Meung, author of a part of the "Roman de la Rose," and which was the prison of François Villon in the fifteenth century. By order of the Bishop of Orleans, the poet was confined here for robbery. He spent one whole summer in a dungeon, which was overrun with rats and into which he was lowered by ropes. His food consisted of bread and water only, and it has been said that he suffered as at no other time in his life. He was released on order of Louis XI, who visited the place and pardoned all prisoners.

Not far from here is Beaugency, a small place with impor-tant sights and several souvenirs of a brilliant past. The Tour de Diable remains from an abbey that was founded in the sixth century. The Tour de César looms above the town, a remnant of the ancient castle. There is an electric railway between here and Cléry. Among the sights are the Hôtel de Ville, the Romanesque church of Notre Dame, many houses of wood and stone, a bridge across the river that has twenty-six arches and a chapel.

CHURCH OF NOTRE-DAME-LA-GRANDE, AT POITIERS, NOTED FOR ITS
ELABORATE FRONT

The region south of Orleans between Blois, Romorantin
and Vierzon is vastly different from what it was in the days
when the lords were erecting their châteaux along the Loire.
Its sandy soil has been drained, and its many small lakes are
now surrounded with vineyards, which flourish like the proverbial green bay tree. The result has been an improvement
in the living conditions of the peasants, who may not be so
picturesque as formerly, but are far more comfortable.
The arrival of the tourist has prompted a desire for better
food, wine, and dress, so that when the farmer of the region
attends the fêtes he now puts on a white collar and prides
himself upon his personal appearance. There is a good stock
of small game, and hunting is the favorite sport. In no
country in Europe, we are told, is there a larger variety of
small game offered than in this part of France during the

open season—towards the close of August or the beginning
of September. But the peasants still cling to many of their
quaint beliefs. It is considered a tragic mistake, I have heard,
to shoot a crow with the first shot, as it is a sign of certain
and sudden death before the day is completed.

The metropolis of the region is La Motte-Beuvron. It may
not have many of the outward appearances of prosperity,
but it has felt the change that has taken place since the
desert of the environs became a garden. The Hôtel de Ville,
said to have been designed after the Arsenal at Venice, was
built by Napoleon III. There is little else to see here, and the
hotels and restaurants cannot be highly recommended.

We reach the ancient city of Bourges, a fine town with
impressive old buildings, over which rises the imposing Cathedral. Bourges is the seat of an archbishop and was the home
of Jacques Coeur, the richest merchant of his time. A distinguished Duke of Berry had been a liberal patron of artists,
and after him Jacques Coeur continued the same protection.
He, Charles VII, and Louis XI often made their residence
here, so that the place has many interesting associations for
one who travels—provided one has the necessary historical
background to realize the import of what he is seeing.

We follow the Rue Moyenne, the chief street of Bourges,
and go uphill to the Cathedral, one of the finest Gothic edifices in existence, specially notable for its west entrance,
double-aisled interior, and priceless stained glass. The archi-
tect is unknown, but it seems likely that his model was Notre
Dame at Paris. The splendid pile was dedicated in 1324.
The western front has five portals and is crowned by two
towers. The tympanum of the central portal has a "Last
Judgment," showing the saved at the gates of Paradise with
St. Peter, and the lost, on the right, being thrown into Satan's

mouth by demons. The two entrances on the right date from the thirteenth century and depict the stories of St. Stephen and St. Ursinus; those on the left are dedicated to the Virgin and St. William. The niches are filled with statues of angels, patriarchs, and saints. The interior is three hundred sixty-two feet long and is lighted by one hundred forty-one windows, including thirty rose windows that have stained glass of the twelfth, thirteenth, fifteenth, and sixteenth centuries, in which about sixteen hundred figures appear. It will be well to make a leisurely tour of the interior, with catalog in hand, or with a guide, as there are many statues, monuments, windows and tombs that are worthy a careful inspection. The crypt dates from the thirteenth century and contains the tomb-statue of Duke John, from his destroyed mausoleum in the Sainte Chapelle.

CATHEDRAL OF ST. PIERRE AT ANGOULEME

The Musée du Berry is in the former house of Jacques Cujas and has many items of historical interest, including: statues of mourners from the tomb of Duke John, the death-mask of Agnes Sorel, portraits of notable citizens, chimney-pieces from old residences; tapestries, furniture, and paintings.

The Palais de Jacques Coeur is usually considered one of the finest extant specimens of medieval domestic architecture. The building, which dates from the middle of the fifteenth century, has its west walls based on the ancient Roman ramparts, and circles an arcaded central court. The entrance from the Place Jacques Coeur has a great gate with a knocker, and above it is a niche that once held a statue of Charles VII, at the sides of which are false windows containing figures of Jacques Coeur and his wife. There is a clock and a fine sculptured turret. We should visit the chapel to see its decorations and the oratories of the owner and his wife. In the keep, there is a carved scene from "Tristan and Isolde."

The Hôtel Lallemant provides a good example of the prosperous citizen of the Renaissance period, and contains several interesting rooms, notably the oratory, which has an elaborately paneled ceiling.

If one happens to be southward bound, it is easy to go from Bourges to Limoges, where the famous pottery is made, and on to Angoulême and Périgueux. Angoulême has a remarkable Hôtel de Ville, built in thirteenth-century style, and a Cathedral that has been called one of the most interesting Romanesque-Byzantine structures in France, recalling those of Poitiers and Périgueux. This curious cropping up of Oriental architecture in the heart of France is especially evident in the Cathedral of St. Front at Périgueux. Many vis-

A BYZANTINE CHURCH IN THE HEART OF FRANCE: ST. FRONT, IN
PERIGUEUX

itors make the journey to that city just to see St. Front and
its foreign-looking eleventh-century tower, the only one of
the kind in France.

A good northerly excursion from Bourges is to Sancerre,
which has winding streets on the hillside that overlooks the
Loire valley. Ascending the hill to the tower, which marks
the seat of the Counts of Sancerre, we obtain one of the best
views of the whole district. The tower remains of the old
Abbey of St. Satur, which once possessed all the lands of the
neighborhood that were not claimed by the Counts. The old
church dates from the fourteenth century and never has
been completed, altho it may be considered a ruin in its
present condition. The English completely sacked the abbey
in 1419, and removed its treasure to boats moored in the
river. The monks were held for a ransom of a thousand

crowns each; and when they protested that there were no funds, as all had been stolen, they were bound hand and foot and thrown into the river, only eight out of fifty-two escaping with their lives. A bloody memory for the English tourist to contemplate as he visits the scene!

Not far from Sancerre is Gien, whose château towers are visible for a considerable distance. This castle was built for Anne of Beaujeu, who was regent of France after the death of Charles VIII. The curious old town repays an hour's visit. It has been called a landmark on Jeanne d'Arc's road to martyrdom, for it was here that she made her plea to Charles VII to march on Rheims.

Literary pilgrims think of the pleasant valley of Berry as George Sand's country, because it was she who made the world acquainted with its pastoral scenes; and one who has read her novels will feel that every turn in the road is familiar territory. The real gateway to the country is Châteauroux, but the native place of the famous writer is Nohant, which, to quote an enthusiast, "as a dainty old-world village is sublime." George Sand frequently expressed her love for the place. There is a pretty old church with a wooden porch, and to the right of it is the novelist's house, in which she spent her last days; in the grounds is the pavilion known as the Théâtre des Marionettes. In a corner of the village cemetery, the spot marked by a mossy stone, reposes the body of George Sand.

We may include the sleepy town of La Charité-sur-Loire, which the French consider one of the picturesque places of the interior, altho it is not frequently visited by foreigners. The town is terraced along the river bank, and many of the stones of the ancient walls repose in the houses of the present. An interesting old place it is, often attacked during the

Hundred Years' War; here Jeanne d'Arc practically met defeat. It was an important scene of the religious wars, and in the sixteenth century, when it capitulated, Henry III celebrated the victory by a fête in which the ladies dressed as men, which caused the fête to be called a "fanatical debauch."

X NORTHERN BATTLEFIELDS

THE SPLENDID GOTHIC CATHEDRAL OF AMIENS CAME
THROUGH THE WAR ALMOST UNHARMED

X

NORTHERN BATTLEFIELDS

THERE are several convenient ways of visiting the battlefields of the late war. Agencies in Paris arrange for conducted tours, which in a way are satisfactory to hurried tourists, because an experienced guide points out the most familiar localities and relates much of interest in regard to what has transpired in the places visited. There are also the tours that may be made to the chief cities by railway and by public conveyance to the near-by points of interest, either with or without a guide. The best way, however, is by private automobile, which permits one to move along as desired, or to linger where there is particular interest, giving the traveler the opportunity to visit several French cities that might otherwise be overlooked—cities that decidedly belong in anything like a comprehensive tour of France.

Traveling in this manner and with plenty of leisure, let us begin our journey at the ancient and important city of Amiens, which, owing to its position on the Somme, was the capital of the Celtic Ambiani and has seen many historic events down through the centuries. In the Middle Ages it was known for its cloth and dyes, the secrets of the latter now apparently lost. The first Bishop of Amiens—in the fourth century—became a martyr. The famous Peace of Amiens was concluded here in 1802 by France, England, Spain, and Holland, but it marked only a pause in the Napoleonic wars.

WONDERFUL CARVINGS OVER THE MAIN DOOR OF
AMIENS CATHEDRAL

In the World War, the city was of great importance as the
main artery of British communications. In March, 1918,
came the sudden crash of the German armies, meant to
separate the French and British and to open the way to
Paris at last. Close by, at Ham and Villers-Bretonneux,
some of the American troops had their first baptism of fire.
The road between the two places was sharply contested by
the Germans and the Allied forces.

Here one seems to plunge into the great conflict, and there
are many souvenirs of war along the way, all of which will
disappear with time and make way for peaceful pursuits.
There remain stumps of trees that were in pleasant groves,
tanks half-buried in the mud, and great scars in the earth

where trench warfare was carried on. The battle of Amiens was a turning-point in the fortunes of the Allied forces in 1918, and Americans helped to win the victory. The Germans had intended this drive as the great "peace offensive," the decisive battle of the war. Over two hundred divisions were assembled under cover of night, and the attack was opened by a sudden belching of guns along a sixty-mile front, while poison gas was ejected over a vast area. Champagne and Picardy were overrun in four days, and the triumphant cry was "Nach Paris!"

Again the Germans were in "the heart of France." Pershing rushed to Foch's headquarters and offered "all I have" in men and munitions. Foch's first plan was to relieve Amiens, and the city was freed from the danger of German spoliation and conquest. It has been written of this time in the conflict: "The Imperial Command had headed straight for military defeat and the suicide of the Hohenzollern dynasty."

Something of even greater interest than the battlefields awaits us at Amiens, and that is the Cathedral, one of the noblest Gothic edifices of Europe and the largest church in France, with an area of eighty-four hundred square feet. It is a magnificent building that marks the height of thirteenth-century architecture. Many of its art treasures were removed to safety during the great struggle; but

A TYPICAL STREET IN AMIENS

they are again in place, and altho the roof was pierced many times during the conflict, much of the damage has been repaired.

One should devote considerable time to a careful inspection and study of this edifice, as it repays close observation. It would be a good plan to walk slowly around the exterior before visiting the interior. The west façade has three portals, with a notable array of statues, statuettes, and reliefs representing religious, allegorical, and symbolic subjects. Above the gallery over the portals are twenty-two statues of the Kings of Judah, ancestors of the Virgin, and above them a rose window of the fourteenth and fifteenth centuries. The central portal has a statue of Jesus on the central pier— a fine work of the thirteenth century—and in the pediment is a relief of the Last Judgment, while one hundred and fifty statues in the vaulting represent the celestial hierarchy. On the gable is a figure of St. Michael. On the central pier of the Virgin Porch is a statue of the Virgin trampling a monster, and in the pediment are her Entombment and Assumption. St. Firnini's porch is dedicated to the saint, represented with idolatry under his feet. The door of the south tower is known as St. Christopher's Gate and has a colossal statue. Between the windows of the chapels are two rows of statues, and the door of the south transept has a graceful figure of the Ma-

CARVED SHOP FRONT IN AMIENS

donna. Between the windows of the nave chapel and on the buttresses are statues of saints and Kings of France. In the porch of the north transept is a statue, supposed to be that of St. Honoré. The Lady Chapel has six seated figures wearing crowns.

BRONZE AND IRON CLOCK-TOWER
IN AMIENS

Simplicity is the keynote of the Cathedral, and the great height, in proportion to the width of the interior, adds to its grandeur. It is four hundred seventy feet long and two hundred fourteen feet wide, and has one hundred twenty-six pillars. The church contains several splendid tombs, and the pulpit is supported by figures of Faith, Hope, and Charity. The transepts have groined vaulting and rose windows. In the south transepts are marble reliefs depicting scenes from the Virgin's life, and above these, reliefs of St. James. On the east side of the altar are statues of David and Judith. Near the font is a relic of the head of John the Baptist, brought from Constantinople in the thirteenth century. The choir is raised above the nave and has wrought-iron railings. There are over one hundred choir stalls, the carving of which represents four hundred scenes from the Bible, trades, and handicrafts. Medallions on the pillars of the sanctuary represent the Evangelists with torch-bearers. The choir screen is elaborately decorated, as are several of the chapels.

We pass the belfry, a strange square tower of the four-

JULES VERNE'S GRAVE AT AMIENS

teenth century, which has a round upper story and a bell that weighs over ten tons. We must not overlook the Musée de Picardie, which contains many rare items. For example, here we come upon the splendid murals of Puvis de Chavannes, which were carried away to Tours for safekeeping during the German bombardment. In this story of the artist and Amiens, we are reminded of the Renaissance, when genius was linked with wealth, power and magnificence, and when princes glorified themselves by glorifying art. The merchant princes of Amiens discerned in Puvis de Chavannes a genius who would add renown to the constellation of French art. Until they bought his "Work" and "Repose," the artist was almost unknown and had suffered from adverse criticism. The attitude of the merchants so encouraged him that the artist gave two paintings to the museum. Amiens adopted him as a favorite son, other works were ordered, and he enjoyed a leisure that permitted him to create many masterpieces while he made the city his residence for seventeen years. He is said to have declared that his paintings in the Pantheon at Paris were his "testament," whereupon it has been commented that his work at Amiens is his "legacy" to France.

The ground floor of the museum has tomb-statues, Renaissance sculpture, weapons, pottery, furniture; prehistoric,

Roman, Greek and Celtic antiquities; sculptures by French artists, and paintings of the French school. Murals by Puvis de Chavannes are on the staircase. On the first floor are examples of French, Dutch, Italian and Spanish art, including some old masters. One room contains thirteen ancient French paintings, the collection of a society that held an annual competition and formerly deposited the prize-winners' works at the Cathedral. The Public Library contains one hundred thousand volumes and fifteen hundred manuscripts.

After we have arrived here and studied the maps, if we have failed to do so previously, we appreciate the vast extent of the entire battle front, which, with its windings and turnings, caused by forward and backward movements, extends over about six hundred miles. Between this and the German front there was the stretch known as "No Man's Land," which

WHERE NEW HOMES ARE BLOTTING OUT THE RUINS OF WAR

varied in width from a few yards in some places to almost a mile in others. Thus we perceive the impossibility of visiting all the territory that figured as "battle-front" in the late war, unless we are prepared to spend much time in the pursuit. Therefore, our method will be to visit cities in the region, and to enjoy them not alone for their connection with the war, but also for their individual attractions, always endeavoring to recall the events that transpired within or near them when they were pivots of world attention in the great struggle.

From Amiens let us go to Arras, a fine old town of less than thirty thousand, which has had a notable history. Centuries ago it was the center of an agricultural region, and before the war it was notable for the production of cereals; but the town now has an industrial appearance. It is

THE HOPEFUL PRESENT VERSUS A TRAGIC PAST

considered one of the "martyred towns" of France, having undergone four years of bombardment by German guns, a record that places it beside Rheims. The Germans captured it in 1914, but were able to hold it only a few days. The Crown Prince established his headquarters at the Citadel and

LILLE SEEN FROM THE CENTER OF THE OLD TOWN

his billet at the Hôtel de l'Univers, where we pause for a cup of tea. Arras never enjoyed even a brief interval of security during the long years of the struggle. Its particular day of horror was October 7, 1914, after the great bombardment of the day before. The beautiful Hôtel de Ville was in flames, and by October 9 the casualties were so numerous that orders were given to burn the bodies of civilians and soldiers as they fell. At the Amiens gate, seventy-two bodies were burned upon a single pyre. For several miles east of the town, one may observe that the old landmarks have disappeared; even the trees that once bordered the roads have been swept away.

In Arras we visit the Petite-Place and the Grande-Place, once the pride of the city, but now shattered; also the Hôtel de Ville, with its famous Gothic façade, completely ruined. Most of the old houses have suffered badly. The Cathedral has Corinthian columns standing in the façade, but the Greco-Roman interior is a waste.

We continue our pilgrimage toward Lens and visit Vimy Ridge, where there are monuments to the Canadians and the Germans who fell in the important engagements. Lens was a prosperous city of thirty-five thousand inhabitants before the war; but to-day it is in a sadly ruined condition, a mass of pathetic reminders of the war's destruction. In the once pretty Place de la République is a mound of débris, marking the site of a church that contained the remains of an English monk named St. Vulgan, who preached Christianity in this region in the sixth century. Lens was important as a coal city, and the destruction of its mines was a great loss to France. The city is making a desperate struggle to regain its former prestige.

From Arras we go to Lille, now an important industrial center and formerly a great frontier fortress. It is still a beautiful city, altho many of the old landmarks have disappeared. Most of us will think of Lille as the place from which "lisle" thread derived its name; and most of us will remember that it was captured by the Germans and that

THE ABBEY AT SOISSONS, IN WHICH THOMAS A BECKET
SPENT NINE YEARS

CLERMONT-EN-ARGONNE, REBUILT SINCE THE WAR

twenty-five thousand of its inhabitants were deported. It was a favorite resort of the Prussian officers, and "leave to Lille" became a German byword, as it was the scene of gay horrors—gay to the invaders and horrible to the inhabitants. All sorts of amusements were provided, and the new theater became a German opera house.

The Hôtel de Ville is in ruins, but there are many buildings that escaped and now hold our interest; for example, the Citadel, a pentagon fortress, which preserves its seventeenth-century aspect, and the University, which is the second largest in France. The Palais des Beaux-Arts is considered the most notable museum in provincial France. About two thousand works of art were removed to places of safety during the war, but they have been brought back and are again visible. The ground floor has sculpture, a collection of

Flemish coins, items illustrating the history of Lille, ceramics, ivories, and wood carvings. The first floor contains the Picture Gallery, some of the treasures of which are: Goya's "Old Women," Andrea del Sarto's "Virgin, St. John and Angels," Paolo Veronese's "Martyrdom of St. George" (a copy of the painting in Venice), Tiepolo's "Donor at the Feet of St. Augustine"; several good examples of Rubens, Van Dyck, Jordaens, Franz Hals, Ruysdael; a portrait by Laurence, a landscape by Constable, a "Fête" by Corot, works by Henner, Cabanel, and Meissonier. The collection of drawings has examples by Giotto, Raphael, Tintoretto, Cranach, Correggio, and Andrea del Sarto. A gem of the gallery is a wax head of a girl, considered by some critics to be of the school of Leonardo da Vinci, and by others ascribed to the time of Raphael.

CHATEAU-THIERRY, WHERE MANY AMERICAN SOLDIERS
GOT THEIR FIRST BAPTISM OF FIRE

Valenciennes, an old town with less than forty thousand inhabitants, is reached in an easy hour's motor-car run from Lille. It gave its name to "Valenciennes lace," which was manufactured here as early as the sixteenth century. Probably the city was named for one of the Roman Emperors named Valentinian. During the retreat from Mons in 1914, the place was abandoned and became headquarters of the German lines of communication for the next four years. Among famous men who were born here are Baldwin, who became Emperor of Constantinople, and Watteau, the painter. The Library has many ancient German and French works. The Hôtel de Ville should be visited; also the Museum, which contains sculptures and paintings of the Dutch, Spanish, and Italian schools, and notably of the French school, including works of Watteau.

STREET IN CHATEAU-THIERRY, REBUILT SINCE THE WAR

THE NEW BRIDGE AT CHATEAU-THIERRY

Cambrai, a prosperous town before the war, had as its chief industry the manufacture of linens, known to the English-speaking world as "cambric" and to the French as "batiste," derived from the name of the inventor, Baptiste Cambray, a weaver of the thirteenth century. When the Germans left the town in 1918, they planted many mines, so that the British entry was succeeded by a series of explosions that destroyed many important buildings in a wide area covering the center of the town. Despite the attacks made upon it, the Hôtel de Ville still presents its splendid façade. Two well-known and quaint mechanical figures, "Martin and Martine," are again in their places in front of the campanile, which we note as we make our way to the Cathedral, formerly the Church of the Abbey of St. Sepulchre. The abbey church succeeded to this dignity after the Revolution

[203]

CHATEAU-THIERRY IS GRADUALLY REBUILDING ITS
WAR-TORN SECTIONS

had destroyed the old Cathedral, which dated from the twelfth and thirteenth centuries. What is likely to interest us most is the tomb of Fenelon—this and a Byzantine painting on wood, brought from Rome in the fifteenth century and popularly ascribed to St. Luke. The museum has a varied collection without any items of particular value or consequence. Modern visitors to Cambrai are chiefly interested in the battlefields near by. Here General Byng made a drive of ten miles that made it appear to the world that the trench system of the Germans had been broken. The Germans, however, organized a counter-drive and came back five miles. The fifth British army had its position near Cambrai when the first German drive came in 1918, and it was badly defeated.

St. Quentin, before the war, was an industrial town with

more than fifty thousand inhabitants, specializing in textile products. It was left prostrate, but has regained much of its lost prestige and activity. The town derives its name from Quintinus, a Christian missionary, who was beheaded here in the third century. It was the capture of this town on St. Laurence's Day in 1557 that prompted Philip II of Spain to commemorate the event by building the Escorial. St. Quentin was also a part of the dowry of Mary Queen of Scots. The Germans entered the town in 1914 and held it until 1918. The second battle of the Somme, also known as the battle of St. Quentin, yielded forty-five thousand allied prisoners in two days, and the Germans advanced fifteen miles. The Hôtel de Ville appears to have escaped serious damage. The Musée Lecuyer, which was completely destroyed, possessed a collection of eighty-seven pastels by the native artist, Quentin de la Tour, which were taken by the enemy but restored after the Armistice and are now in the Louvre at Paris. A fine promenade, known as the Champs-Elysées, is a feature of the city's life. The spacious Church of St. Quentin was badly damaged by bombardment, but was reopened in 1920. It is one of the finest Gothic churches in France. Its choir screen has bas-reliefs from the life of the saint, whose body, with those of his companions, reposes in the crypt.

Compiègne is an ancient town on the Oise, which has many associations with French kings and was notable as the site of the Benedictine monastery of St. Corneille. Making a sortie from here in 1430, Jeanne d'Arc was captured by the Burgundians, who sold her to the English. In Compiègne, Marie Antoinette was received by Louis XIV and Marie Louise by Napoleon. The Germans occupied the town in 1914, but retired in a few days, before the Allied advance.

MEMORIAL TO THE AMERICAN SOLDIERS WHO DIED AT CHATEAU-THIERRY

The Armistice was signed at Rethondes in November, 1918, only four miles east of here. Near the end of the old bridge, which was blown up in 1914, is the spot where Jeanne d'Arc was captured. It is marked by a tablet. The Hôtel de Ville has a pretty façade, adorned with graceful statues. The tower has a bell cast in 1303 and a sixteenth-century clock, which every fifteen minutes sets in motion wooden figures known as "Picantins." The interior of the building contains a small museum of objects representing the fine arts and a few drawings by old masters.

Our chief object of interest at Compiègne, however, is the Château, designed under Louis XV and restored by Napoleon. The façade has a graceful portico, looking toward the terrace and park. The interior contains much furniture installed by Napoleon. The Galérie des Tapisseries, a series of eight apartments, contains magnificent Gobelins: "The Story of Esther" and "The Story of Jason and Medea." The chairs have Beauvais tapestry. The Galérie des Fêtes is in white and gold and has statues of Napoleon and his mother. The state apartments face the park and we visit the bed-chamber of Marie Louise. The music-room has tapestries, and the library a desk of the Emperor; the bedroom of Napoleon has an odd-shaped bed and an Empire clock. The table in the small dining-room was used by Napoleon on his campaigns. The park is a beautiful wooded expanse leading to dense forest. A trellis-walk on the north side was constructed for Marie Louise, to remind her of a similar decoration at Schönbrunn in Vienna. The little park, below the terrace, has a small formal garden with sculptures. The large park, to which there is no admission, is reserved for official shooting-parties. The vast Forest of Compiègne is often considered the finest wooded tract in northern France.

METHODIST MEMORIAL AT CHATEAU-THIERRY

About twenty-four miles away is Soissons, an ancient fortress and a cathedral town, which, like so many of its neighbors, suffered greatly during the war. Reading its history, however, one realizes that it has been used to warfare over a period of fourteen centuries and the wonder is that it has survived at all; yet to-day it is a busy market for agricultural products. In the Middle Ages it was often besieged and it suffered during the Hundred Years' War. Even in 1870 it fell under a three days' bombardment. The Germans held the town in the early days of 1914, and when they left they destroyed the bridges. There were other engagements here, and in May, 1918, the invaders came again after they had rushed through Chemin-des-Dames, and the town was not again liberated until August, when the gunners played havoc with the ruins.

The Hôtel de Ville stands upon the site of a former castle of the Counts of Soissons and contains the public library and a museum of antiquities. The secularized Abbey of St. Leger has been badly damaged, as has been the Gothic Cathedral, which dates from the thirteenth century. The south transept, in which service is held at the present time, dates from the twelfth century and always has been considered the most beautiful portion of the church. The ruins of the once important Abbey of St. Jean-des-Vignes, founded in 1076, are still worth a visit. Thomas a Becket resided here for some time. The façade of the church, about all that remains, bears a resemblance to that of Rheims Cathedral. The Abbey of St. Medard, on the right bank of the river near the former bridgehead, is said to be where Louis the Debonair was imprisoned by his sons. About one-half mile north of the town is the Abbey of St. Crépin-en-Chaye, said to have been built on the exact spot where Saints Crispin and Crispinian were martyred in the year 297.

About ten miles northeast of Soissons is the celebrated Chemin-des-Dames, a name familiar to American newspaper readers in the days of the Great War. This "Ladies' Road" was constructed for the daughters of Louis XV between Compiègne and the Château de la Bove. The Allies were in a firm position here in May, 1918, but the Germans made a surprize attack and captured thousands of prisoners.

We next visit Laon, a town of about sixteen thousand, beautifully situated on a hill that overlooks the surrounding plain. The Cathedral is perched on the summit of this hill, and is considered one of the best among the secondary churches of France. It escaped the war with slight injuries. From the western tower, project figures of huge oxen, perhaps, as claimed, a tribute to the animals that dragged the stone for the construction up the hill of their own accord and without being driven. The façade is elaborately decorated.

Of most importance to Americans is a visit to Château-Thierry, where at the near-by Belleau Woods our marines and doughboys had their first baptism of fire. The Germans were on the Marne when American troops were hurried from Paris to stem their efforts to cross. Casualties were heavy, and ambulances in a steady stream were soon on their way to Longchamps racetrack in the Bois at Paris, where thousands of American wounded were placed in tents and such medical attention as was then possible was given by a staff of American doctors and surgeons.

I happened to be in Château-Thierry at the time, and I shall never forget the unexpected and hurried attack, in which I was the victim of a minor casualty that for ten days rendered me hors de combat. Our boys made a wonderful stand. They were up against superior numbers of well-trained and experienced troops, but succeeded in driving the Germans back and saving the day for the Allies.

Later I returned to Château-Thierry when the period of reconstruction had brought from a mass of charred ruins a semblance of the former city. An American memorial dedicated to our engineers had been erected on the bank of the Marne. So accustomed had the inhabitants of the city become to our doughboys and tourists that a sign in a window announced: "English spoken, American understood."

In the cemetery at Belleau Woods thousands of our boys, who made the supreme sacrifice, lie in rows, their graves marked by marble and granite headstones.

XI RHEIMS AND BEYOND

VERDUN, ALONG THE RIVER FRONT, HAS RESUMED ITS OLD PLACID LIFE

XI

RHEIMS AND BEYOND

RHEIMS possesses a jewel of architecture as rare and beautiful as almost any city can boast. To see it alone would be reward enough for the journey to France, were the city and its environs of no particular interest. Rheims, however, is in the midst of a delightful region of vine-clad hills, and there is a remarkable history attaching to the place that cannot fail to stir the heart of the sentimental visitor who looks upon the beauties of the present and contemplates the glories of the past. It has been said that the titles alone of the books that have been written about Rheims Cathedral would fill an entire page of closely printed type. From the earliest visitors to those of the present have come a stream of tributes and observations; it has not been enough to see and admire—there has been an almost universal desire to publish the good news, to invite the world to come and feast the eyes upon this "frozen music," this miracle in stone.

Cæsar was at Rheims two thousand years ago. The city was Christianized in the third century, but the Vandals and Attila endeavored to lay it low. It endured, however, and raised its head in pride and importance. Down through the ages, similar events have transpired; but always with the same result. Rheims is again in a period of recovery and convalescence, after holding the place of honor among the martyred cities of France; again it is renewing its strength,

RHEIMS CATHEDRAL IS SLOWLY RECOVERING FROM ITS
GRIEVOUS WOUNDS

and the magnificent edifice that is an inspiration to all mankind still sits proudly upon its foundations and is undergoing restoration that will attempt to make it what it was before German guns attacked its fair face.

The famed saint of the city is St. Remi, and after 816, up to the Revolution, every king of France was consecrated by Remi's successor—with the exceptions of Louis VI and Henry IV. Here Jeanne d'Arc stood holding her white banner beside Charles of Valois as he swore to make the Church secure and to rule France with mercy and justice. In 1694, the earliest newspaper of France was printed here. It is claimed that the earliest aviation meeting ever held took place here in 1909. In 1870, the city was occupied by the Prussians, and in September, 1914, almost exactly forty-four

[214]

years later, the Germans began to rain shells upon Rheims and its Cathedral—a bombardment that lasted for years, and practically destroyed the entire town. The civilian population was evacuated; but it is chronicled that about seventeen thousand inhabitants remained in the city. The vast wine cellars became an unexpected protection, and they "carried on," maintaining schools, courts, and a newspaper, even during Easter week of 1917, when more than twenty-five thousand shells fell on Rheims. The city, indeed, was shelled every day for a period of four years and one month. It is said that at the close of the war less than one hundred houses remained intact, while nearly one thousand were completely destroyed. The material damage at Rheims has been estimated at $370,-000,000. But, as all the world knows, Rheims and its beautiful Cathedral survive!

HOW RHEIMS IS BLOTTING OUT HER WAR MEMORIES

[215]

John Buchan, in telling the story of the shelling of Rheims Cathedral, which he condemns as an act of vandalism unjustified by any military necessity, says in his "History of the Great War":

"To the French it appeared a happy omen that the statue of Joan of Arc, which stood in front of the Cathedral, was uninjured. Round it the Uhlans had stacked their lances when they first entered the city on their way to the Marne. During the bombardment, tho the square around was plowed up by shells and her horse's legs were chipped and scarred, the figure of the Maid remained inviolate. Some soldiers had placed a tricolor in her outstretched hand, and in all these days of smoke and terror the French flag was held aloft by the arm of France's deliverer."

Let us go at once to this royal church of France, one of

IDEAL NEW HOMES OF WORKMEN IN RHEIMS

ONE OF THE NEW HOTELS IN RHEIMS

the noblest Gothic edifices in the world. It has scars upon
its beautiful face, but the main fabric is being restored, and
visitors are admitted. The archbishopric of Rheims was
founded near the beginning of the third century by St.
Sixtus; but the earliest church building was not erected upon
this site until the fifth century. Clovis was baptized here
in 496. The present structure was begun in 1211, and the
west towers were not completed until 1430. On the steps
of the Cathedral are two captured German guns, hardly
symbols of peace, but under the circumstances considered
appropriate souvenirs. The west front has an elaborate array
of sculpture. There is a triple portal; the central doorway,
dedicated to the Virgin, includes groups representing the
Annunciation, the Visitation, and the Coronation. The right
doorway is flanked by statues of the Prophets and sur-

RHEIMS RESTORED: NEW BUSINESS BLOCKS AND WAR MEMORIAL

mounted by a Last Judgment, badly damaged. The left doorway is dedicated to the Passion, and at the left of the door is the decapitated figure of the "Sourire de Reims," an angel, which has become a venerated symbol of the people. Above the rose window are David and Goliath, Saul, Solomon, and the Apostles. High up between the towers is a group representing the baptism of Clovis, and the centerpiece contains huge statues of the Kings of France. The north façade is decorated with statues of former bishops, and on the tympanum are scenes from the lives of St. Nicasius and St. Remigius.

The west end of the interior has one hundred and twenty statues. The pillar capitals are carved with foliage. Some of the works of art belonging to the church have been returned since the war; but others are still missing. The collection includes: rare tapestries representing scenes from the life of Clovis, fourteen tapestries representing the life of the Virgin, other tapestries showing Biblical scenes; paintings, including a "Christ and Mary Magdalen," sometimes ascribed to Titian; the Chalice of St. Remi that was used by the French Kings at their coronation mass; a reliquary made for the coronation of Charles X, and Roman mosaics.

The archbishop's palace, near the Cathedral, has been almost entirely destroyed. The Museum contains a collection of paintings, some of which are by Millet, Fromentin, Ziem, Rousseau, the two Cranachs, and Holbein the Younger. From here we go to the large Abbey Church of St. Remi, which dates from the eleventh century (thus the oldest church in Rheims); it stands upon the site of the Chapel of St. Christopher, erected in the cemetery where St. Remi was

WAR RUINS AND NEW CONSTRUCTION IN A VILLAGE NEAR VERDUN

APPROACHING VERDUN: ANCIENT TOWER GATE AND BRIDGE
ACROSS THE MEUSE

buried. The church was badly damaged during the war. Behind the altar is the reconstructed mausoleum of St. Remi, which contains his reliquary and is decorated with statues of twelve peers of France in their coronation robes, taken from the original tomb.

Doubtless it will be of great interest to visitors to inspect the vast wine cellars at Rheims, where it is possible to gain first-hand knowledge of the processes by which champagne is made. In this city there are over seventeen miles of these galleries. The Hôtel de Ville was destroyed by bombardment, and the subsequent conflagration destroyed its library of one hundred thousand volumes. In the Place de la République stands the Porte de Mars, a Roman triumphal arch believed to date from about the third century. Rheims has a fine new hotel, every room with a private bath.

Several excursions to the battlefields may be made from Rheims, as much of the surrounding territory was devastated during the war. Trips may be made by light railway to Asfeld, Beine, and Cormicy, in case one is not traveling by private automobile. Some of the villages and localities made familiar to newspaper readers from French dispatches were: Berry-au-Bac, Brimont, Nogent-l'Abbesse, Fort de la Pompelle, Grandpré, Rethel, Mezières-Charleville, Revin, Fumay, and Givet.

From Rheims we may go to Sedan, which has been tersely described as the scene of the French disaster of 1870 and of the Allied triumph of 1918. In the closing stages of the battle of the Meuse and the Argonne, the Americans succeeded in gaining the left bank of the river and a suburb, but the Citadel and the major part of the town remained in

VERDUN'S NEW SHOPS ARE BUILT WITH TASTE

A NEW STREET IN VERDUN, BUILT ON THE RUINS WROUGHT
BY GERMAN GUNS

MEMORIAL THAT NOW COVERS THE "TRENCH OF BAYONETS"

German control until the
signing of the Armistice. Less
than three miles away by
train, we reach Bazielles, notable in the battle of 1870.
Here is a historic inn that has
many relics of the battlefields.
The cemetery has a pyramid
covering a crypt in which
three thousand French and
Prussian soldiers are buried.

THE TRENCH OF BAYONETS
Where each rifle is in the dead hands
of a soldier buried by German shells

Verdun is one of the an-
cient fortified cities of France.
The very name still has a thrill
for the whole world on ac-
count of the important events that occurred here during
the Great War. Verdun has been a place of vast consequence
to Europe for many centuries, as it was the Treaty of Verdun
that divided the empire of Charlemagne among his three
grandsons and laid the foundations for the modern kingdoms
of western Europe. Mention of the city can be traced back
to at least a century before the beginning of the Christian
era, and down through the ages the near-by countries have
contested for its possession. It is written that in the year 450
the hosts of Attila left it "like a field ravaged by wild beasts."
We see the scars of the latest war on every side; but restoration measures are being taken, and Verdun, like so many
other French cities, is making long strides toward regaining
its lost prestige.

First of all we go to the Cathedral, which is of Rhenish
character. Portions of it date from the twelfth and thirteenth centuries. The roof was destroyed in 1917 and is

GENERAL VIEW OF NANCY, LOOKING TOWARD THE HANDSOME GOTHIC CHURCH OF ST. EPVRE

being repaired. One obtains a fine view of the battlefields by ascending the northwestern tower. The first church on this site probably dated from the fifth century and was founded by St. Pulchrome upon the ruins of a Roman *castrum*. It was destroyed and rebuilt, damaged and restored, and is said to have been greatly altered at least ten times, so that to-day it does not rank high for its architectural grace.

The Citadel occupies the former site of the Abbey of St. Vanne, founded in the tenth century. The tower, which dominates the river, was used as a wireless station during the war and thus became a target of the German gunners; but its walls were a safe shelter, and several important military conferences took place here. The battlefields extend from the Argonne Forest to the Meuse, and the hills on the north were violently contested. The bombardment obliterated all landmarks of the region; still, if one's time is limited, or if there is a desire to see only one "typical" battle-torn district, it is advisable to make this selection and to join one of the motor-bus parties that go out from Verdun, or to make the circuit by private automobile, which may be engaged in the city. In a military cemetery here lie seven "unknown soldiers," brought from various battlefields; the eighth is the official "unknown," who lies beneath the Arc de Triomphe in Paris. One should include the surrounding forts at Verdun and the Tranchée des Baïonettes, now a military shrine.

Next we visit Chalons-sur-Marne, usually considered an important military city as well as a center of the wine trade. It is another ancient town that was an episcopal see as early as the third century, its bishops ranking as peers of France. Wool cloth made here was referred to by Chaucer as "chalouns." Near here, in 451, Attila and his forces were defeated by the Romans. The town was occupied by the Germans in 1914 and was retaken by the French a month later. It was the chief objective of the fruitless German attack of July 15, 1918. The Cathedral is mainly of the thirteenth century, but its Romanesque tower is from an earlier church. There are interesting monumental slabs in the pavement of the interior, and the stained glass is worth seeing. The Museum has a small collection of pictures, including works by Franz Hals and Daubigny, natural history specimens, and weapons of the last war.

Bar-le-Duc is picturesquely situated in a narrow valley between wooded and vine-clad hills. Its chief sight is the fifteenth-century Church of St. Pierre; it contains the tomb of René de Chalons, Prince of Orange, which is surmounted by a ghastly sculpture representing the body in decay. It is a pleasant little town, nevertheless. Americans know Bar-le-Duc chiefly through the delicious preserves of that name, made of the currants and gooseberries from the sunny hillsides of this region.

Those who choose to take the short run from Bar-le-Duc to Toul will find there two noteworthy churches—the old Gothic Church of St. Gengoult, with a lofty interior, and the former cathedral, St. Etienne, with a beautiful front flanked by two light and graceful towers. The cloisters adjoining both of these very old structures are worth going far to see.

St. Mihiel ranks high in modern history as the scene of the great American victory of September, 1918. The capture by American troops, in thirty hours, of a salient which the Germans had successfully held against all French attacks for four years, was an event that stirred the world to enthusiasm. One authority has written: "The Staff and Army of the United States had demonstrated its efficiency, beyond the shadow of a doubt, and at the same time won its spurs. There could be no longer a question as to the justice of the American contention that its armies were on a par with those of France and Great Britain. German propaganda could no longer successfully deny that the Americans had 'arrived' and their success raised the morale of the Allied troops to the highest pitch."

NANCY HAS SEVERAL CHARMING
PUBLIC SQUARES

The name of the town is derived from that of St. Michael, and it was around this saint's ancient abbey that the town developed. The abbey was founded in the year 709 and conducted a school that became celebrated. The town had about seven thousand inhabitants before the war; but it has few monuments of interest to the visitor who does not make the trip to the battlefields. One of its most famous sons was Ligier Richier, the sculptor, who has several works scattered

HOW NANCY HONORS A
LOCAL HERO

about the town, notably the "Entombment," in the church of St. Etienne, which has thirteen statues.

· Metz was the German capital of Lorraine and it is now the principal town of the French department of the Moselle. Usually it is considered the most formidable fortress in Europe, and it has been a place of vast strategical importance for two thousand years. Julius Cæsar describes it as one of the oldest towns in Gaul. The older parts of the town still have narrow streets; but there are broad boulevards in the newer parts, all of German construction; the German names of these drives have been changed since the war, many of them in honor of Allied generals and statesmen. There are at least three gates of the old city walls that should be seen. There are many attractive walks about the place and pretty views from the terrace of the Moselle Valley. The Cathedral of St. Etienne is a late-Gothic building that contains notable stained glass. It occupies the site of a circular church, and parts of it date from the thirteenth century. The façade has statues of prophets; one of these, Daniel, bears a striking resemblance to Wilhelm II, and in 1918 it was decorated with the legend, "Sic transit gloria mundi." The huge bell is said to weigh ten tons; and the exterior of the church has many flying buttresses between the pointed windows. Inside, we observe many interesting monuments and tombs; a large porphyry basin of Roman origin, once used as a font; a Graouly figure of a dragon that took daily toll of the inhabitants of Metz until it was captured and drowned by St. Clement (mentioned by Rabelais), and an interesting crypt. The Museum has antiquities and a small picture gallery.

Nancy is a fine city of over one hundred thousand inhabitants, with beautiful squares and avenues; everything in it indicates prosperity and refinement. The place is built about the castle of the ancient Dukes of Lorraine. Much important history has been made here, and it is interesting for its souvenirs of the past, as for its present attractions. Many of its embellishments are due to Stanislas Leczinski, ex-King of Poland and father-in-law of Louis XV, who became Duke of Lorraine for life and who held court here, attracting many famous persons. During the last war, the town was bombarded and attacked on several occasions, but its scars are not so evident as are those of many other cities upon which the Germans cast envious eyes. The Cathedral, which was converted into a Temple of Reason during the Revolution, is not an imposing building. The Place Stanislas is enclosed by buildings of uniform design—the Hôtel de Ville, the former episcopal palace, the theater, and an excellent restaurant. In the middle is a monument of Stanislas. The Museum has a good collection of paintings, some of the best being: "Virgin, Child, and St. John," by Perugino; Rubens's "Transfiguration," from a Mantuan church; Ribera's "Baptism of Christ," Andrea del Sarto's "Tobias and the Angel," water-colors, pastels, and miniatures. Facing the Hôtel de Ville is the Porte Royale, a triumphal arch in honor of Louis XV. The Ducal Palace is a Gothic building, begun in the fifteenth century, which contains the Musée Historique de

Lorraine, with antiquities, tapestries, iron work, and souvenirs of Napoleon. Near the Museum is the Franciscan Church, dating from the fifteenth century. It contains the tombs of the Dukes of Lorraine. To the west of Nancy is the Cure d'Air St. Antoine, on the borders of the fine Forest of Haye, which covers sixteen thousand acres on the plateau between the Meurthe and Moselle.

From Nancy we may go to Dijon, a city of about eighty

ONE OF THE ARCHITECTURAL TREASURES
OF TOUL

thousand inhabitants and an important industrial town, center of the Burgundy wine trade. It was fortified by Marcus Aurelius and converted to Christianity in the second century by St. Benignus, in whose honor an abbey was built in the sixth century. The Cathedral is of Burgundian Gothic, succeeding a Romanesque basilica, the chief doorway retaining features of the twelfth-century structure. The most notable secular building is the Hôtel de Ville, formerly the palace of the Dukes of Burgundy, and it is erected upon Roman foundations. It contains the Museum, chief exhibits of which are: sculptures on the ground floor, enamels, ivory and glass, a "Virgin and Child" by Leonardo da Vinci, sketches by old masters, Perugino's "Virgin and Child," tombs of the Dukes of Burgundy, altar-pieces, Franz Hals's "Laughing Child," Andrea del Sarto's "St. John," Tintoretto's "Assumption," Rubens's "Descent from the Cross," and Gainsborough's "Old Man." The Church of Notre Dame should be visited, not alone for its mural paintings of the thirteenth century, fine sixteenth century glass, and "Assumption" group in the sacristy, but particularly for the "Black Virgin," which has been much venerated since the beginning of the sixteenth century.

There are many sights around the city that will reward the pedestrian who has no set route, but merely wanders and keeps his eyes open. For example, the Palais de Justice, which dates from the days of Louis XII and was intended as the meeting-place of the Burgundian parliament; the streets of quaint old houses, the church of St. Michel, the Place du Président Wilson; the Library, which contains as one of its treasures a portion of a fifteenth-century breviary; several parks, monuments, the Botanical Garden, natural history museums, and promenades. About half a mile from the center of the city stood the Chartreuse de Champmol, founded by Philip the Bold in 1383 and intended as a burial-place for the ducal house. It was lavishly decorated by contemporary artists, but few of the treasures have survived; most important of those left is the "Well of Moses," a pedestal rising from a well and once doubtless the base of a Calvary. It is surrounded by statues of Isaiah, Moses, David, Jeremiah, Daniel, and Zachariah; above them, a prediction of the death of Jesus, and figures of angels. The well is of remarkable size, being twenty-three feet in diameter.

About fourteen miles south of Dijon is the Abbaye de Citeaux, from which the Cistercian order derives its name. It was founded in 1098 and owes much of its importance to St. Bernard, who came here with his brothers and assisted in the foundation of four "sister" abbeys. The communities rapidly increased in numbers, so that within a century from its founding, the order had one thousand monasteries in Europe and Palestine. The Abbaye de Citeaux is now private property, but visitors are admitted upon application.

XII STRASBOURG UNDER THE TRICOLOR

GRAND OLD STRASBOURG CATHEDRAL, WHICH THE WAR RESTORED
TO FRANCE

XII

STRASBOURG UNDER THE TRICOLOR

THE city of Strasbourg, which before 1914 seemed to be a typical German city, has undergone an almost miraculous change. Germany insists that this miracle cannot be performed in the Tyrol, where Mussolini is endeavoring to make Italians of a German population. Time alone will tell. At any rate, the French have accomplished it at Strasbourg. Several years after the war, the city was as German as ever. Waiters at the hotels and restaurants spoke French conspicuously when a guest entered the establishment; but they quickly inquired, "Verstehen Sie Deutsch?" and if they received an affirmative answer, they were pleased and the guest received far better service. They said that Strasbourg would not be French before another generation; but they were mistaken. To-day, one finds it as typically French as the Parisian boulevards. All the shop signs are in the French language, and so are the advertisements on the tramcars and buses, and the menus at the restaurants and hotels. The visitor hardly hears a word of German, unless he announces that he understands that language and cannot understand French. German has become a concession or courtesy to visitors; French is the official and almost the universal language. It is considered not so "polite" to speak in German.

The principal stores have taken on a chic that is typically French and never observed in Germany, even in the metropolis. Paris newspapers are the popular reading of the people. The streets in the center of the town are filled with little iron tables and chairs, where people spend hours, sipping coffee or cordials, and gossiping about the affairs of the day. One observes a few beer-drinkers; but they may be seen anywhere in France. Even citizens of German ancestry (particularly the younger generation) appear to enjoy the innovation. Probably they had a smattering of French before the war, for many of the population understood and spoke both languages; but now they seem to chat loudly in the cafés to prove their fluency in the French tongue.

The leaven has worked. Often it is a slow process; but there has been speedy accomplishment at Strasbourg. It seems that all that remains untouched of this typical old German city is its Cathedral and its manufacture of *pâté*

A GLIMPSE OF STRASBOURG, FACING "LA PETITE FRANCE" RESTAURANT

de foies gras. A monument has been erected to the inventor of Brie cheese; Strasbourg, without any such stimulation of publicity, still pays tribute to the goose. A china model of a goose is in half the shop windows of the place. The goose appears in gold, silver, and enamel souvenirs of the city. Strasbourg remains the greatest center of the goose-liver industry in the world.

The birds are artificially stuffed with food, so that their livers become distended, and the product, garnished

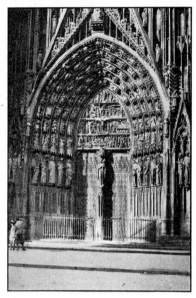

ENTRANCE TO STRASBOURG
CATHEDRAL

with truffles, is sent around the world, and—in America, for example—the price is almost that demanded for jewels. Geese are raised by the thousands in the neighborhood and gorged with food by artificial means—all to make a Roman holiday for the epicurean world. The *pâté* is placed in fancy jars, like Astrakhan caviar, and Strasbourg reaps the harvest. In the city itself, prices of this delicacy, like the prices of most other things, are not high. The last time I was there, I had a large room and bath at a leading hotel for $2.40 a day. I attended the opening luncheon at a huge restaurant and had a meal costing sixty cents that one could not purchase for less than three or four dollars in a similar establishment in America. There were six courses of delicious food, splendidly served. For eighty cents I bought a jar of *pâté*

THE ALSATIAN MUSEUM IN STRASBOURG

that costs $2.50 in an American delicatessen shop; but these prices are now materially higher.

To the usual traveler Strasbourg means, first of all, a visit to the Cathedral. This is one of the magnificent edifices of the world; altho huge in proportions, it is also lace-like, and the stone of which it is built is like a carved cameo. It required the work of four centuries to complete this beautiful Gothic monument, which stands upon the site of an edifice built by Clovis and rebuilt by Charlemagne. At the time of my last visit to Strasbourg, I went to the Cathedral in the afternoon, when there were many tourists chattering and pattering throughout the vast enclosure. But for the sound of the organ and the distant chanting of priests, the place seemed less a church than a huge ecclesiastical relic under the control of a government bureau at Paris—a colossal souvenir of the past that must be preserved for the future. In the evening, I went back to obtain a view of the delicate stone tracery by moonlight (when all Gothic structures seem most beautiful and awe-inspiring). As I stood there gazing upward, an American approached and we exchanged greetings. He was in Strasbourg for the purpose of obtaining photographs of sculptured details of the splendid western façade.

"I experienced a shock to-day," he related, as he pointed to a large building across the street. "There is where they preserve the originals—that is the Church Museum." This was somewhat confusing, so I asked him to elucidate. "Yes, I felt about it just as you will," he continued. "Unfortunately, stone decays. It is the way of the world, and had it not been for restoration and for what we must call loving as well as scientific and intelligent reproduction, we should not behold the beauty that we now see. The wonderful façade before us is—almost stone for stone—a faithful reproduction of the original. The work has been going on for years—even centuries—and I have been told that but for restoration, the great central piers of the interior might have toppled, leaving only a huge ruin, instead of the edifice that we admire. Millions of francs have been spent to preserve the Cathedral, and altho the world which views and admires it is unaware of the fact, what we see to-day is almost a rebuilt structure. The original statues are carefully measured and photographed, and duplicates take their places when they are carried to the Museum. I wonder how long governments will continue to make appropriations for this purpose. It seems to me that buildings like these belonged to the people who constructed them, and that the devotion of such people is necessary for their ultimate maintenance."

The western façade has a wealth of statues, and, with its "veil of delicate tracery," rises to a height of two hundred and sixteen feet. The huge rose window is fifty feet in diameter, and there are three portals, the central one having bronze doors embellished with bas-reliefs. Statues of the Wise and Foolish Virgins decorate the side portals, and above them are statues of ancient Kings. The Apostles appear above the rose window, and surmounting all is the Last Judgment. The beautiful spire is decorated with statuary and flanked by four turrets, above the highest of which is the lantern, topped by a stone cross, which rises to a height of four hundred and sixty-four feet. The southern portal has the Coronation of the Virgin in the tympanum and groups representing Christianity and Judaism.

The interior of the Cathedral reveals a vast nave and fine

AN OLD PALACE IN STRASBOURG, WITH THE CATHEDRAL SPIRE
BEHIND IT

stained glass as its outstanding features. The carved stone pulpit is considered a masterpiece. St. Catherine's chapel has a very old wooden altar with panels showing the Visitation and Annunciation; the Chapel of St. Mark has ancient windows. In the south transept is the celebrated Astronomical Clock, which reveals the calendar, the position of the planets, the courses of the sun and moon, and moves a series of allegorical figures of the Four Ages of Life, in procession before Death, which strikes the hours. The Twelve Apostles appear at the stroke of noon and pay homage to a figure of Jesus, whereupon a cock crows three times and flaps its wings.

The Musée des Beaux-Arts occupies the former Château de Rohan, residence of Cardinal de Rohan, which was purchased by Napoleon and restored to the city by Louis-Philippe. The picture gallery holds an interesting collection, some of the chief features of which are: a "Madonna," by Tiepolo; Ribera's "Sts. Peter and Paul"; Rubens's "Saviour of the World," "St. Francis," and "Visitation"; Jordaens's "Peasant Festival"; Rembrandt's "Head of an Old Man"; Claude Lorrain's "Flight into Egypt"; Corot's "Lake of Ville d'Avray"; a landscape by Ruysdael; "The Walk," by P. de Hooch; six altar panels by Hans Memling; cartoons from the studio of Leonardo da Vinci; German, Swiss and Alsatian primitives; wood-carvings, and stained glass. The Museum of Decorative Art, in the same building, contains jewelry, bronzes, faience, and the keys of the city presented to Napoleon in 1806.

The Musée Historique de la Ville has objects relating to the history of Strasbourg from the Middle Ages to the entry of the French troops in 1918. Not far from the museum is the house in which the poet Goethe lived when he was a student. We visit the Church of St. Thomas chiefly for

WHY FRENCHMEN LOVE FRANCE: A SUMMER DAY IN A FRENCH PARK

the purpose of seeing the tomb of Marshal Saxe, which was built on the order of Louis XV. The Marshal is represented descending the steps of a pyramid of gray marble, at the foot of which is his coffin, while France endeavors to detain him and Hercules mourns his earthly rival. The church became a store or granary at the time of the Revolution, and it is said that the tomb escaped mutilation by being covered with hay. There are several other tombs in the church, some of them enclosing embalmed bodies, a carved stone coffin, and some good stained glass. There are several other old churches that we may like to visit: the Wilhelm Kirche, founded in 1300 for the Guillites; St. Etienne, a thirteenth-century basilica, and St. Pierre-le-Jeune, founded in the eleventh century, with a fine rood-screen and baptismal fonts.

On the rectangular promenade known as the Place Broglie, dating from 1740, at number two is the Maison de la Marseillaise, the house in which Rouget de Lisle sang the "Marseillaise" for the first time on April 25, 1792, as recorded upon a tablet. The Rue Brulée or Brandstrasse is named from the burning of two thousand Jews, who were accused of poisoning the city's wells in 1348. The University (founded in 1566) occupies an imposing palace and is now a home of Gallic culture, having two thousand French and many foreign students.

The port of Strasbourg is the head of navigation on the Rhine. It is the fifth in magnitude among the ports of the river, and has elaborate docks for the accommodation of shipping.

There are several interesting excursions to be made from Strasbourg. About eleven miles distant is Molsheim, an ancient town lying beneath the vine-clad hills at the foot of the Vosges. Here are several splendid old houses and the remains of medieval fortifications. The parish church was founded for the College of Jesuits in the sixteenth century. The old Hôtel de Ville is an interesting building, and it is well to note that the wines from this district are held in high esteem among connoisseurs.

From here we may go to Rosheim, an old fortress with well preserved ramparts and several fine views. Obernai is a picturesque town, partly walled, which has a good Hôtel de Ville and pretty chapel. It was the residence of ancient Dukes of Alsace, and here is the house where St. Odilia was born. Barr is a popular summer resort. Its ancient Hôtel de Ville is a former castle of the bishops of Strasbourg. There are several picturesque drives from here, during which several castles may be seen, and there are traces of Roman

POLICE HEADQUARTERS IN COLMAR, ALSACE

potteries in the region. At Andlau is a Romanesque church—the restored remains of a convent for noble ladies, founded in the ninth century by Richarda, said to have been the wife of Charles the Fat. St. Nabor is the station for the Convent of St. Odilia, an important place of pilgrimage, where the nuns offer hospitality to visitors. The convent was founded in the seventh century by St. Odilia, the patron saint of Alsace, who was blind at birth, but who received her sight at baptism. It was abandoned in the six-

PFISTER HOUSE, COLMAR

teenth century, but was re-occupied by the sisters of the third order of St. Francis in 1853. In the church are the reliquary of the saint, her former tomb, the tombs of her parents, and other relics. Probably those familiar with the "Ingoldsby Legends" will recall the "Lay of Odille" when here.

Taking the route from Strasbourg to Colmar, if we are going to Bâle, we pass through Erstein, a factory town, which has several old houses. Benfeld is a small place with less than three thousand inhabitants, but it was mentioned as the villa of the bishops of Strasbourg as early as the eighth century. At the village of Ebermünster is the "monastery of the wild boar," once the seat of a celebrated abbey said to have been founded by the father of St. Odilia. Selestat,

A DISTINCTIVE CITY HALL—IN COLMAR, ALSACE

one of the ancient towns of Alsace, was an early residence of the Frankish Kings. Erasmus is said to have been a student at the academy here, afterwards having a great influence upon the revival of learning in Alsace. It is claimed that the art of glazing pottery was discovered by an unknown citizen of the town. The Church of St. Foy is a fine edifice erected in the eleventh century. In its crypt is a reproduction of the Holy Sepulcher and a bust of Princess Hildegarde, one of the founders. The head and bust of the princess are said to have been discovered in a perfect state of preservation. A pleasant excursion from Selestat is to the famous castle of Hoh-Koenigsbourg. The city presented this castle to the late Kaiser, who ordered it restored—at public expense. It dates from the fifteenth century, with parts reaching back to the twelfth century, and there are varied collections within its chambers. We come next to Ribeauville, which is famous for its white wines and its "three castles on one hill"—the ancient stronghold of the Ribeaupierre family, the castle of Girsberg, and the castle of St. Ulrich.

Colmar has about thirty-five thousand inhabitants and is an attractive city at the foot of the Vosges, with some picturesquely timbered and painted houses. In the eighth century, the place was known as Columbaria, when it was the farm of the Frankish Kings. The Museum here is worth a visit on account of several items, chief of which is the collection of panels by German primitives. These panels were removed to Munich for safety during the war and restored in 1919. In the collection of moderns are works by Henner, Doré, and Vernet. The Church of St. Martin is a Romanesque structure of the tenth century. It has some good stained glass and several unusual features, including official measures of length, one of which is known as the "ell of Colmar." The altarpiece shows the "Virgin in a Bower of Roses," which also was removed for safety in wartime and later returned. A pretty excursion from Colmar is to Kayserberg, a picturesque town, notable for its Hôtel de Ville of the German Renaissance, its parish church with interesting sculptures, old houses, and ruins of an abbey church. A motor-bus runs regularly between Colmar and

GABLE VIEW OF CITY HALL, MULHOUSE

the pleasant summer resort of Orbey, which suffered considerable damage during the war. It is not far from Colmar to Turckheim and to Les Trois Epis, a favorite resort of the Vosges, which has grown up around an ancient pilgrimage convent. At Rouffach, if we have no other association to interest us, we shall think that it was the birthplace of Marshal Lefebre, the miller's son who became Duke of Danzig,

BUSINESS CENTER OF MULHOUSE, IN SOUTHERN ALSACE

MULHOUSE, LIKE COLMAR, BOASTS A DISTINCTIVE CITY HALL

and whose wife was the original from whom Victorien Sardou drew the amusing portrait of "Madame Sans-Gêne."

Mulhouse is considered the industrial capital of Alsace, being specially noted for its hardware and textiles. The only relic of the old city is the Hôtel de Ville, which is covered by strange mural paintings that date from the sixteenth century. There is an exterior covered stairway; also a "gossips' stone," carved in the shape of a head, hanging on

THE LION OF BELFORT, CARVED IN RED SANDSTONE
BY BARTHOLDI

the front. It is said that persons convicted of gossip were condemned to parade the town, on a market or fair day, with this stone dangling from their necks.

If we are journeying to southern France or to Paris, instead of Switzerland, we go to Belfort, a city of forty thousand inhabitants, with a first-class fortress. It is the principal town of the so-called Territory of Belfort, which remained to France after the annexation of 1871. The small city of Lure is situated in a thickly wooded country and owes its foundation to the seventh-century abbey of St. Desle, an Irish monk. Then on to Vesoul, the native city of Gérome the painter, whose memory is much honored by his townsmen. The Museum contains many of his works—including his famous "Tanagra"—and a monument with a bust of him by Carpeaux.

It may please us to stop for a day in the small city of Langres, which was an ancient city of allies of Cæsar. One of its rulers was Sabinus, who endeavored to form a Gallic empire shortly after Nero's death in A. D. 68. A church was founded here in the second century, and from the twelfth to the eighteenth century its bishops were peers of France. It was the headquarters of the Chief of Staff and the training school of the American army in France in 1918. Concerning this school, an authority has written: "Our soldiers had to

PROMENADE AT VITTEL, A FAVORITE HEALTH RESORT
IN NORTHERN FRANCE

study the new methods of trench warfare and the use of gas, and had to practise the dodges used in cleaning up trenches and throwing grenades. We were supplied with equipment we lacked. Our artillery was insufficient; the French let us have enough artillery to equip thirty divisions; but it is worth remembering that not one piece of divisional artillery from the United States had reached the front by the date of the Armistice."

XIII LYONS AND BEYOND

BASILICA OF NOTRE DAME DE FOURVIERE, ONE OF THE
MANY FINE CHURCHES IN LYONS

XIII

LYONS AND BEYOND

MAKING our way southward, we arrive in Lyons, the third city of France, situated at the confluence of the Rhone and the Saone; a city that lies on the hillsides, and yet has twelve miles of docks and quays. Its fortifications are said to be fifty miles in length. It is the headquarters of an army corps, the center of an archiepiscopal see, and the seat of a university, thus one of the most important cities of the country. It has a history that stretches back over the centuries to a time before the Christian era; Christianity was preached here in the second century, and the city was favored by the Emperors until after the invasion by the barbarians, after which it had many rulers and finally was given over to a King of France in the fourteenth century. After having been practically destroyed, the city arose from its ruins under Napoleon, and then entered upon a period of prosperity that has continued until the present. Lyons to-day is considered the world-center of the silk industry, with one hundred and fifty thousand workers.

Assuming that we enter the town by way of the Gare de Perrache, we go to the Place Carnot, where there is a monument of the Republic, a bronze statue preceded by a figure of the City of Lyons and surrounded by Liberty, Equality, and Fraternity. In the Place Ampère is a statue of the famous physicist, and beyond the square is the Church of

St. Martin-d'Ainay, probably one of the oldest in France, as it was founded in the sixth century. The local legend is that it stands upon the site of a school founded by Caligula. The façade is richly decorated, and a tower is supported by four large antique columns. The mosaic inscription in the choir observes that the church was consecrated by Pascal II in 1106.

The finest square in the city is the Place Bellecour, which has an equestrian statue of Louis XIV. This is a popular promenade, and near by is the best residential quarter of the city. One of the public buildings most worth seeing is the Palais de la Bourse et du Commerce; its heavy façades have huge pavilions with pointed roofs, and the square court inside has windows flanked with caryatids in wood. Under the porticos are the Elements and the Seasons, and the clock

WHERE THE SAONE FLOWS THROUGH LYONS TO JOIN THE RHONE

HOTEL DE VILLE, LYONS, WITH BARTHOLDI FOUNTAIN ON THE RIGHT

has statues of the Hours. It was in this building in 1894 that President Carnot was assassinated. The second floor contains the Musée Historique des Tissus, in which are textiles and embroidery made before the seventeenth century, Oriental lace, and textiles; also tapestries, pictures in silk, and a special library.

The Place des Terreaux, the most important in the city, with the possible exception of the Bellecour, is laid out upon the site of an ancient Roman canal between the Rhone and the Saone. In it we find the Fontaine Bartholdi, named for the sculptor of the Statue of Liberty in New York harbor; the fountain with which Lyons has honored him contains huge figures of Rivers and Springs flowing toward the sea. The Hôtel de Ville has a richly decorated façade with many sculptures, and behind it rises the clock tower. The interior should be visited for its tapestries, chimney-pieces, and other relics of the bygone.

The Palais des Arts is a building of the seventeenth century formerly belonging to Benedictine nuns, and its court has been made into a public garden. The Sculpture Gallery has some rare items, chief of which are Mino da Fiesole's bust of John the Baptist, an "Angel and Boy" from the school of Donatello, a "Madonna" ascribed to Andrea della Robbia, Cortot's "Pandora," Delorme's "Mercury," and Chinard's "Perseus and Andromeda." The Picture Gallery was founded by Napoleon. The Salle des Dessins has a bust of Puvis de Chavannes by Rodin and notable works by Lyons artists. The Collection of Antiquities has bronzes, terra-cottas, vases, a Venus of the sixth century B. C. with a dove in her hand, ancient utensils, and mosaics. The Museum of

REAR VIEW OF THE HOTEL DE VILLE, LYONS

Medieval and Renaissance Art has some good examples of Italian bronzes, wrought iron, Limoges enamels, Oriental weapons, plaques, churchware, Swiss porcelain, and furniture. The Library is located on the first floor and contains a collection of thirty thousand engravings and some first-rate manuscripts. The second floor has a continuation of the Picture Gallery, containing such gems as: Ruysdael's "Norwegian Scene," Rubens's "Saints Francis and Dominic Saving the World from the Wrath of Christ," Jordaens's "Adoration of the Shepherds," Paul Potter's "Landscape with Cattle," Rubens's "Adoration of the Magi," Ribera's "Saint in Ecstasy," Perugino's "Ascension," Tintoretto's "Madonna and Child," Paolo Veronese's "Bathsheba" and "Finding of Moses," LeBrun's "Thanksgiving of Louis XIV," Courbet's "Happy Lovers," J. F. Millet's "Naval Officer," Greuze's "The Charitable Lady," Courbet's "Deer," a Corot landscape, and a Rigaud portrait.

CATHEDRAL OF ST. JEAN, LYONS

Over on the right bank of the Saone is the Cathedral of St. Jean, which was begun in the twelfth century, and the façade of which has three portals and has been denuded of its statues. The bell weighs nearly ten tons and is one of the largest in the country. The windows have splendid old stained glass, and we should not fail to visit the Chapelle St.

FOURVIERE HILL, LYONS, WITH NOTRE DAME AT TOP AND PALAIS DE JUSTICE IN THE FOREGROUND

Louis, which owes its existence to the Cardinal de Bourbon. There is a clock that dates from 1598 and plays at frequent intervals during the day. Not far away is the Church of St. Paul, said to have been founded in the middle of the sixth century. For a comprehensive view of the city, we should ascend by funicular railway to the Hill of Fourvière, which has two churches that are a favorite resort of pilgrims. One contains a black image of the Virgin and walls covered with votive offerings. Notre Dame de Fourvière is a massive edifice consecrated in 1896. It has a gallery from which the city is blessed on September 8 each year. The façade has large granite monolithic columns supporting a gallery with angels, over which is a sculptured pediment. Blue-gray marble columns divide the nave and aisles. The interior is decorated with mosaics and paintings. There are ten red marble columns in the choir, and the altar is constructed of valuable materials.

On the left bank of the Rhone are the University buildings and the Prefecture, the latter in a pretty garden. The Parc de la Tête d'Or contains nearly three hundred acres, a lake with islands, hot-houses with good collections of tropical plants.

Among the many excursions that may be made from Lyons I would recommend the pretty steamboat ride on the Saone to Ile Barbe, during which one obtains an intimate view of the picturesque country life of the region. On the island there are ruins of a convent, a chapel, and a castle, and here are held religious celebrations at Easter and Whit-Monday. About five miles west of the city is Charbonnières-les-Bains, another popular excursion. The place has a cold spring and a casino. It takes about three hours to go from Lyons to Bonnaud and see its famous Roman aqueducts with

PROMENADE ON THE QUAI ST. CLAIR, LYONS

LAKE TETE D'OR, LYONS, IN THE PARK OF THE SAME NAME

eighteen arcades, or further along to Chaponost, where there are ninety arcades.

From Lyons it is a short journey to St. Etienne, an important town that is the capital of the department of the Loire, in the great coal fields of which it is situated. It manufactures many things, among them firearms and hardware; but one of its specialties is ribbon, an industry

BIRDS OF A FEATHER

that has flourished here for three centuries. Immediately, we are impressed by the lively appearance of the streets, which are animated and much more colorful than those in many of the towns of interior France. There are only a few "sights," as the tourist usually thinks of such things, but to the observing visitor everything is a sight, and one may obtain here an excellent impression of the entire population of the region. Among the buildings of St. Etienne, our attention is first attracted to the Hôtel de Ville, a modern building with a dome surmounted by a lantern; on its steps are iron statues of Metallurgy and Ribbon-Making, the two great industries of the place. The Palais des Arts will interest us for its various collections. On the ground floor, the Artillery Museum shows primitive weapons, firearms, armor, and cannon. The Library has an interesting collection of books and manuscripts relating principally to art and industry. The stairway leading to the first floor has paintings by Glaize and Fragonard, and engravings. The Picture Gallery has many modern paintings, coins, tapestries, and furniture. The In-

[263]

LAC DU BOURGET, WHICH LENDS AN ADDED CHARM TO AIX-LES-BAINS

dustrial Museum has models of looms, embroideries, and a collection of silk stuffs and ribbons.

St. Etienne is no more interesting than various places that are easily reached from it in short excursions. For instance, the journey to Mont Pilat, one of the chief heights of the northern Cevennes. Its legend is that Pontius Pilate killed himself here, in remorse; but we are told the same thing at Pilatus on Lake Lucerne, whereas the truth seems to be that he ended his days in Rome wholly unaware of his future reputation, and, according to Anatole France, entirely forgetful of the tragic event in which he played such an important part. There is a popular saying in the region: "When Pilat puts on his hat, put on your coat." The summit of Mont Pilat offers a view on a clear day that is ample reward for the ascent, as one is able to see the Alps in the east, the Rhone valley, the southern Cevennes, the Auvergne hills, and the Lyonnaise hills to the north.

From St. Etienne it is comparatively easy to go by train up into the most picturesque portions of the Cevennes Mountains, and to see the deep canyons worn into the *causses* or limestone plateaus by the age-long action of the waters of the Lot, Tarn, Jonte and other streams in their descent from the glaciers of the Cevennes.

Especially well worth seeing are the Gorges of the Tarn, which are easily reached by motor-bus from Mende, on the railway. The gorges begin at the village of Ispagnac and extend past Ste. Enimie to Le Rozier—thirty miles of canyons, at times more than a thousand feet deep, between the cliffs of the Causse de Sauveterre on the one side and the Causse de Méjan on the other. The trip from Ste. Enimie by boat on the Tarn is a memorable experience. Only in the Alps has France anything to compare with these picturesque gorges. The beauty of the scene is increased by its variety, for in some places it consists of gigantic ramparts overhanging the river, and in others, less precipitous, abundant vines and fruit trees afford a charming contrast to the shattered blocks of yellow limestone.

There is a pleasant excursion from St. Etienne to the Barrages, which provide water for the city in a reservoir containing nearly three hundred million gallons. Motor-cars

ARCH OF CAMPANUS AT AIX-LES-BAINS

run on certain days to the Grand Bois, a fine pine wood. Or from St. Etienne we may like to visit Vichy, one of the most popular watering-places in France, which attracts nearly one hundred thousand visitors each year. The old town, which is uninteresting to visitors, dates from the Middle Ages; but the new town is entirely modern. The Vichy waters were known to the ancient Romans. Madame de Sévigné introduced them at the court of Louis XIV, and they became fashion-

A CHARMING CITY IN A BEAUTIFUL SETTING: AIX-LES-BAINS

AIX-LES-BAINS AT THE HEIGHT OF THE SEASON

able also during the Second Empire. There is a daily supply from all the springs of about sixty-four thousand gallons. The casino with its gambling, the thermal establishment, the parks and promenades add to the attractiveness of the place for visitors, as do the many de luxe hotels.

From Lyons there is a convenient route to Aix-les-Bains, one of the most famous spas in France, which owes its popularity to its warm sulfur springs. These springs were known

THE SOLARIUM, AIX-LES-BAINS, WHERE PATIENTS
ARE TREATED WITH SUNSHINE AND VIOLET RAYS

to the Romans, but the place passed into a decline during the Middle Ages and again began to attract visitors in the seventeenth century, the number increasing until now about thirty-five thousand strangers are entertained here each year. The height of the season is in summer, when numerous first-class hotels are open to receive the throngs. The "cure" is considered particularly efficacious for rheumatism and skin diseases. The great rendezvous of visitors is the Etablisse-

CHAMBERY'S QUAINT CATHEDRAL IS EIGHT CENTURIES OLD

ENTRANCE TO THE CASTLE AT CHAMBERY, WITH MONUMENT
TO JOSEPH AND XAVIER DE MAISTRE

BOIGNE COLUMN, CHAMBERY

ment Thermal, a fine modern bathing establishment, which is open the year round and is supplied by two copious springs. In front of the building is the Arch of Campanus, a monumental gateway supposed to have been the entrance to a burial-place of the third or fourth century. The Hôtel de Ville, once the château of the Marquis d'Aix, has some interesting antiquities of the lake-dwellings of Lac du Bourget, and Roman inscriptions found in the region. The

building is said to occupy the site of a former temple of Venus or Diana. The so-called Grand Circle dates from the days of public gaming and is now the scene of fêtes and concerts.

Marlioz, another spa, has a pretty park and sulfurous springs, the waters of which are more popular for drinking than those of the better-known neighboring city. Only about two miles west of the town of Aix is Lac du

RUE HECTOR BERLIOZ, GRENOBLE

A VIEW TO INSPIRE ANY ARTIST: ON THE QUAI
CLAUDEBROSSE AT GRENOBLE

Bourget, magnificently situated in the mountains, conveniently visited by motor-bus. Steamers make the circuit of the lake
several times daily during the season, and it is worth while to
visit the Cistercian Abbey of Hautecombe, which has a chapel,
the burial-place of the Princes of Savoy from the twelfth to
the eighteenth centuries. Another popular excursion from
Aix is to the Gorges du Sierroz, which we may visit by motor-
bus in season. Other popular drives are to the Colline de
Tresserve, Le Bourget, Bourdeau, and the Col du Chat.

It is only a short distance from Aix to Chambéry, an interesting old town and once the capital of Savoy. During the
war it was a favorite place for recuperation of sick or dis-
abled American soldiers.

Grenoble is a splendid fortress of the first class and a city
of close to eighty thousand inhabitants. It has an unusual

IN THE PLACE NOTRE DAME AT GRENOBLE

position at the junction of the Drac and Isère and is defended by a complete enceinte. High mountains in close proximity make it a popular center for tourists, and it seems to have been in great favor from the earliest times. It was the ancient Cularo, and the Romans called it Gratianopolis for the Emperor Gratian, who founded the bishopric in the fourth century. It has been the scene of notable religious wars and has survived many important events of history. One of its leading activities is the manufacture of kid gloves, an industry that is said to employ twenty-four thousand hands in the district of which it is the metropolis.

Probably the most interesting building in the place is the Palais de Justice, with a façade that is an excellent example of the early French Renaissance. We should visit the interior for the purpose of seeing the splendid sixteenth-century wood-carving by Paul Jude, a German sculptor. From the northern façade we go to the Quai de la République, which affords some admirable views of the city and its environs. The Cathedral of Notre Dame is an edifice dating from the eleventh to the fifteenth centuries, not particularly attractive on the exterior, but having inside a fine stone tabernacle forty-five feet high. In the apse are gilt reliefs of scenes from the life of Mary. In the Place Notre Dame is a monument of the Revolution, and opposite the Cathedral is the Tour de Clérieux, which commands another fine view for a long distance.

The Museum deserves a visit, as the Picture Gallery contains several items of the first rank, and the Library is a treasure-house of valuable books and manuscripts. Among the paintings, we admire: Paolo Veronese's "Jesus Healing

EVERY BEND OF THE SWIFT-FLOWING TARN OPENS UP A NEW PICTURE

CAMPING ON THE CEVENNES MOUNTAINS, IN THE GORGES
OF THE TARN

WHERE THE MOTOR ROAD WINDS THROUGH THE
GORGES OF THE TARN

the Woman" and "The Risen Christ Appearing to Mary Magdalene," Canaletto's "Venice," Tintoretto's "Madonna with Saints and Donor," Murillo's "Young Cistercian Monk," Ribera's "Martyrdom of St. Bartholomew," and Rubens's "St. Gregory," which was carried off from Antwerp by Napoleon; also Jordaens's "Adoration of the Shepherds," Fantin-Latour's portrait of himself, a landscape by Harpignies, Courbet's "Waterfall," Delacroix's "St. George," and Ravier's "Rising Sun."

There are many excursions from Grenoble that await the tourist who has the leisure to enjoy them. Several are particularly inviting to the pedestrian, others may be accomplished by private auto or motor-bus and others by tram and train, making the city the center for all and spending the nights there. The tramway runs to La Trouche, and it is interesting to climb to the fortified St. Eynard, which affords an excellent view. Another tramway runs to Sassenage, a pretty village, whence we may go to the Gorges du Furon, with attractive waterfalls. From Seyssinet, we may ascend to the Château de Beauregard. It is about eight miles to Uriage, a pretty village notable for its mineral waters from an abundant spring in a pretty park. The water was known to the Romans and is still said to be efficacious in the cure of nervous disorders.

Perhaps the best route to the Grande-Chartreuse is by way of Voiron, St. Laurent-du-Pont, and thence by motor-bus. The monastery was founded by St. Bruno in the eleventh century and usually is referred to as the cradle of the widespread order. Its prior was the superior of the order, and when the law of 1901 dissolved nine other houses, state recognition was requested for the Grande-Chartreuse monastery, but it was not granted and the monks were expelled

in 1903 and removed to Italy; so the monastery ranks as a
"national monument" and has not the interest of the olden
times, altho it repays a visit. Visitors are admitted and are
escorted to the chapter-house, the Chapelle St. Louis, the
library, the prior's parlor, and the cemetery, where it was
the custom to bury the monks without a coffin and face
downward. We also obtain here a good idea of what a Carthusian monk's "cell" was like; he was forbidden to talk and
only permitted to see his associates on Sundays and certain
feast-days. Beyond the Grande-Chartreuse are numerous
excursions that are delightful.

From Grenoble, it is convenient to visit the Gorges
d'Engins, the Grand Arc, the Gorges de la Bourne, and the
Gorges de la Vernaison, all of which afford beautiful scenery.
Or we may go higher into the Alps, the chief attraction for
many visitors to Grenoble; to La Mure, Allevard, Briançon,
Oz, Allemont, Belledonne, several glaciers, Vallouise, or
Digne. The time spent here will depend upon one's leisure;
one may linger days or weeks in the environs of Grenoble
and obtain a satisfactory impression, or may make the region
the locale of an entire summer's excursions and thoroughly
enjoy each hour. It is one of the most beautiful parts of
France, and while well known to European visitors, it is too
often overlooked by Americans.

XIV DOWN THE RHONE

VIENNE WAS THE CAPITAL OF BURGUNDY IN THE MIDDLE AGES

XIV

DOWN THE RHONE

ONE of the delightful experiences of a journey through France is the trip down the Rhone, starting from Lyons, reserving sufficient leisure to stop wherever there is a desire to do so, and going along as there is an impulse to move toward the south. The Rhone has been called a majestic river and merits that word, which is often thoughtlessly used. It is not only majestic, but it also offers a variety of scenery on both sides as the boat turns at every bend, and one appreciates the landscape all the more as one drifts closer and closer to the sub-tropical brilliancy of the sunlit portion of France, a region admired by all the world.

Here we know that we are entering the country of Frederic Mistral, who wrote the "Poème du Rhône," a fascinating work descriptive of the life, manners, and landscape by one who was close to the soil and loved the region, and who could pour out his soul in a manner that has caught and held the attention of all readers.

"In the bed of the Rhone," he writes, "thickset with islands, the sun throws its warmest radiance upon the little whirlpools which shine as they revolve and lose themselves in each other as they boil up, and upon the thickets where rise the white poplars, with their high naked trunks, white, round and polished, as if they were the thighs of some gigantic nymph or goddess. Verdant turf stretches between

the osier-beds and the river; warblers innumerable utter their
strident cries in the reed beds. . . . Like shining plates of
steel, the long and gloomy waves lull us to sleep, almost to
intoxication. And the arches of the bridge of Saint-Esprit,
prodigies of architecture, pass triumphantly above their
heads. Provence appears, for its gateway is the bridge of
Saint-Esprit with its piles and its twenty proud arches, which
curve like a crown across the Rhone. It is the holy gate, the
gate of triumph, of the land of love. The olive tree, the
pomegranate in the pride of its flowering, and the millet
with its great bearded heads, already adorn the slopes of the
hills and the marshy flats. The plain expands before us; the
copses are green in the clear light, the heavens have the glory
of Paradise."

It is small wonder that we launch forth upon this river

A QUIET COUNTRYSIDE WATERED BY THE RHONE

ST. MAURICE CATHEDRAL AT VIENNE

with the keenest anticipations. Less than twenty miles from
Lyons, we arrive at Vienne, a fine old town that lies at the
confluence of the Rhone and the Gère. It was the Roman
Vienna Allobrogum and was a colony of importance under
the Empire. It was the seat of a long line of archbishops,
who held the title of Primate of Gaul in recognition of the
fact that the city was a cradle of Christianity. One of them
became Pope Calixtus II. A quick glance at the town to-day
gives one the impression that it is chiefly interested in commerce and industry; but a second glance reveals ample evidence of its remote antiquity, which is likely to interest us
more, as visitors, than the factories and the bustle that are so
important to the living residents of Vienne. First of all, we
may visit the Cathedral of St. Maurice, a Gothic church
built between the twelfth and sixteenth centuries. The choir

[281]

DRIVING A HARD BARGAIN

has a green marble altar and the tombs of archbishops; sculptured groups of the "Adoration of the Shepherds" and "Herod and the Magi" are near the aisles at the portals, while at the sides of the main portal are the sarcophagi of St. Leoninus and the Archbishop Aymar.

Next we go to the Temple of Augustus and Livia, which dates from about 41 A. D.—in the reign of the Emperor Claudius. It is ninety by fifty feet and fifty-seven feet high, the façade having six fluted columns and the other sides five. This structure usually is ranked second to the splendidly preserved Maison Carrée at Nimes. The inscription has been deciphered from the socket holes of the old letters and probably read: "To Cæsar best and greatest, the divine Augustus, Emperor, and to the divine Augusta." Portions of the ancient Roman forum are visible and there is a fascinating gateway that leads to the theater. Not far from the river is an interesting pyramid, concerning which there has been much archeological speculation. Certain students have maintained that it was the turning-point in a circus, but there are no other remains of such a structure. Others have believed it to be a tomb and still others a war memorial erected by Fabius after his victories. It is in reality an obelisk resting upon a portico, with an arch at both sides.

Ste. Colombe-les-Vienne, connected with Vienne by a bridge, has an interesting old church, which contains good pictures and a marble group called "The Education of the

Virgin," dating from the fifteenth century. St. Pierre is one of the oldest Romanesque churches in France, parts of the walls dating from the fifth century. Its walls are supported by antique marble columns, and now, much restored, the edifice houses the Musée Lapidaire.

"At Valence the South commences," said Thiers, truly. Valence, the Roman Valentia, picturesquely situated upon the left bank of the Rhone, is a splendid old town with a

TOOT! TOOT! FRESH VEGETABLES!

notable history. Its bishopric dates from the fourth century, and the bishops ruled the city for several centuries. It became a duchy for Cæsar Borgia, and Diane de Poitiers was the titular duchess in the sixteenth century. Its Cathedral of St. Apollinaire was consecrated by Pope Urban II in the eleventh century, and while it has been frequently restored, it is still a building of great interest to visitors. It contains a monument to Pius VI, who died in exile in the Citadel. There is sufficient interest in several of the old buildings, but

[283]

A NOBLE RELIC OF CÆSAR'S WARS IN GAUL: THE TRIUMPHAL ARCH AT ORANGE

still more interesting are the numerous excursions that may be made from Valence as a base. One of the best of these is to Die, the Dea Vocontiorum of the Romans, probably dedicated to Cybele, and one of the chief colonies on the road from Milan to Vienne. The chief relic of the ancient town is the Porte St.-Marcel, erected in honor of Marius. The Cathedral has a porch with four splendid granite columns that appear to have belonged to a temple, perhaps one dedicated to Cybele. The esplanade near the Hôtel de Ville has a bust of the Countess of Die, who lived in the twelfth century, a poetess beloved by a troubadour of Orange.

We enter Provence at Montelimar and pass through interesting territory to the ancient and splendid city of Orange. It is here that we may come upon the "terrible mistral," the north wind of the Rhone valley, which seems to have been exaggerated by many famous personages; for example, by Madame de Sévigné, whose letters might give one the impression that it is always blowing. Altho the mistral is general all along the southern boundary of France, it does not always blow for the proverbial six or nine days; and when it comes in summer it makes these southern cities cool and healthful. It is the reverse of the sirocco of the African desert, which makes the cities on the European side of the Mediterranean such delightful winter resorts.

We have entered one of the most-talked-about regions in the world and should recall that Provence in the Middle Ages comprised a more extensive territory than at present. Even in Roman times it was referred to as "the province," so the name became official and remains a proper noun. There was a brilliant civilization here in the twelfth and thirteenth centuries, which resulted in what may be called almost a new literature; it set the fashion for the court poets and the troubadours, who occupy an important place in French chronicles. The small courts became "courts of love," presided over by ladies of distinction, who established a code of "women's rights" far in advance of the time.

We arrive at Orange, a fascinating old city, which was of importance in Roman days, as some of the ancient monuments prove. Among these, we come first to the Arch of Triumph, which usually is considered the finest monument of its kind in France. Its exact age is unknown, but it is inferred from the name of Sacrovir on one of the shields, that its erection followed the defeat of this chieftain in A. D. 25, and the date is further strengthened by an inscription to Tiberius. The structure was a stronghold in the Middle Ages, and we see it now in the state to which it was restored in 1825. It has three arches with splendid vaulting; the outward side has four fluted Corinthian columns, and the attic is elaborately decorated with battle scenes. On the sides are trophies and figures of captives.

Chief of the remains of Roman glory, however, is the Theater, whose huge façade still dominates the town to-day, altho the structure dates from the second century of our era. Entering by a small door, we come upon an amphitheater seating seven thousand spectators, now a "National Theater" in which performances are given each August by notable actors. Those August days are notable in Orange, on account of the large number of visitors attracted to the city. A hill lies back of the theater, and on it are a statue of the Virgin and the ruins of a château built of Roman materials for the Princes of Orange.

Here we have a reminder that most of the great buildings of the Romans were devoted to pleasure. Theaters and arenas seem to occupy entire cities, and yet, in their present ruined condition, we have but an inkling of what they were in the ancient days. This provision for ample amusement was the policy of the imperial authorities. The mob in the provinces, as at Rome, was not easy to control; but the rulers had learned that if it was entertained it was likely to be harmless. As a result came the great baths, some of which occupied enough area for a small city. Some of the halls were as large as modern cathedrals; there were gossiping-rooms, music-rooms, libraries, galleries of pictures and sculpture, galleries for gymnastics and games, gardens and arcades. When the people tired of quiet amusements they went to the arenas for gladiatorial contests, witnessing bloody scenes in which captive slaves had to fight with hungry beasts, and other exhibitions that were prophetic of the fall of a people who found delight in them.

BROKEN BRIDGE OVER THE RHONE AT AVIGNON

Visitors who have enjoyed seeing these Roman remains at Orange should make the excursion to Vaison, about seventeen miles away. The ancient theater at Vaison is smaller than the one we have just seen, but the town was of great importance in Roman days, and there is ample evidence that the whole place was magnificently ornamented by statues, several of which are visible to-day. The city museum has several of these, besides funeral urns, pottery, glass, lamps, and marbles that once formed the background of the theater stage. The town has remains of four antique baths.

The Cathedral of Notre Dame, at Vaison, dates in its various parts from the seventh to the eighteenth century. It has a strange inscription running around its exterior, now almost obliterated, which someone has believed to be: "I beg you, brothers, forego all that makes for evil by following the cloister, because thus you will come into the South. Let the position of these stones remind you that the warmth of heaven from three sides strikes upon the four sides of the cloister, a warmth that is given to the twelve veins." This inscription is a puzzle to the archeologists, and the age of the building itself is a puzzle to the architects, some of whom believe it dates from the beginning of the Christian era. The Church of St. Quentin, not far from the Cathedral, also is worth visiting.

Another excursion from Orange brings us to Carpen-

PALACE AND CATHEDRAL, AVIGNON

tras, now an industrial town, but of great historical importance, as proved by its Arch of Triumph and Cathedral. The reliefs of the former show slaves bound to trophies, a warrior clad in sheepskin, and a soldier with a battle-ax.

Avignon is the city of the Popes, and here we should pause as long as possible, because there is much to see and we shall profit if we explore the city in leisurely fashion. A glance will not suffice, as in

ANCIENT RAMPARTS OF AVIGNON

other cities; but the visitor who has arrived here will need no encouragement from me to prolong his stay. The difficulty is to make up one's mind when to leave, and when the day comes one has the feeling that much remains unseen. Avignon is one of the many places in Southern France that give the visitor a thrill and make him wish to return. The palatial city is not Provence, any more than Paris is France; but one could not afford to miss it. It is picturesquely situated and impressive as one approaches it; the population is about fifty thousand, but one's first impression is that it must have at least the eighty thousand that it had in the fourteenth century, when it was the official residence of seven Popes, from Clement V to Gregory XI. Avignon was an important Roman colony, but its ancient splendor could not have compared to that of the medieval days, when the spiritual head of the Roman Catholic Church resided here, surrounded by a splendid court.

When Clement V made Avignon the papal capital, he

[289]

THE PAPAL PALACE AT AVIGNON: VIEW SHOWING THE MAIN ENTRANCE

probably had no idea that it was to continue as such for any great length of time; but when it became apparent that the place was to be the papal stronghold, Benedict XII erected the first of the buildings that were to become the Palace of the Popes. In those days it was necessary to give the place at least the appearance of a fortress, if it was to last; but within, the palace resembled a large monastery with a cloister around the square court. It was called at one time the finest building in France, for while it had a monastic appearance, it was adorned by the best Italian artists.

Avignon became the chief center of the councils, and the various orders of the church established their headquarters in the city, which profited greatly by events as they transpired. The city became so crowded that it was extremely difficult for visitors to obtain lodgings, and even the ambassadors were obliged to stay at Villeneuve or other near-by places. People came in flocks from all parts of Europe—architects, painters, and money-changers from Italy—and the Germans established their own fraternity. The relatives of the Pope arrived, and the ladies of the family were accorded special privileges; for example, they were permitted to wear ermine and gold jewelry. At the entrance to the papal apartments there were special guards, porters, and several sergeants-at-arms. The Pope had thirty chaplains, attendants galore, a special group of learned men under a master of theology, many cooks, stewards and secretaries, men who tasted the wine that he was to drink, a special official in charge of the fruits to be served at dessert, others to look after a large stable of horses and mules, messengers to carry papal orders and letters, barbers, doctors—probably about four hundred persons connected with the court—so that John II was said to have spent three million francs in a single year for the maintenance of his household. Finally, each Cardinal had his palace, each order, guild, and confraternity its home. The confraternities were associations of pious people who desired to live after the Christian rule and prove their religion by works of mercy. At least seven of them were situated in Avignon and operated with papal sanction.

The visitor to Avignon naturally goes first of all to the Palace of the Popes, a castle with walls thirteen feet thick. It was used as barracks from 1822 to 1906 and has undergone extensive restorations. It was a prison during the Revolution, and Napoleon III attempted restorations at the expense of the state. We enter the so-called Court of Honor and come to the Audience Chamber, once adorned with frescoes by an Italian artist, of which nineteen figures from the Old Testament and a sibyl remain. A staircase leads to

EXTERIOR OF THE ANCIENT ARENA AT NIMES

[292]

the Grande Chapelle. The Tour de la Garde-Robe has frescoes of hunting and fishing, and the Tour des Anges contained the treasury, the bedroom of Benedict XII, and the library. We visit chapels, the dining-room, and other rooms, one of which, the Tour de Trouillas, is said to have been the prison of Rienzi in 1352.

The St. Peter's of Avignon is Notre-Dame-des-Doms, situated on a rock north of the Palace; it is said to have been founded in the fourth century, but the present building dates from the twelfth century and frequently has been restored. There are rich decorations in the interior, including splendid marble balustrades. In the choir is the marble papal throne, which attracts our attention, as does the supposed tomb of Benedict XII; but the chief glory of the edifice is the tomb of Pope John XXII, a splendid work of the fourteenth century. The Pope's statue has been replaced by the figure of a bishop under a Gothic canopy.

Behind the Cathedral we come upon the Promenade du Rocher-des-Doms, extending to the verge of a cliff which descends abruptly to the river. Here is a bronze statue of Jean Althen, a Persian, who introduced madder into France, a root used in the dyeing of French military trousers and greatly remunerative to the district until it was superseded by cheaper dyes in 1871. Here we obtain a fine view of the Rhone and the distant mountains; also of what is left of the celebrated Pont d'Avignon, which was built across the river in 1177-85 under the guidance of St. Bénézét. We visit the Church of St. Didier, which dates from the fourteenth century, and the Church of St. Pierre, which has a pretty pulpit with statuettes that may have come from the tomb of John XXII. The church also contains ten pictures of events in the life of St. Anthony of Padua and other interesting pictures

WHERE ALPHONSE DAUDET WAS
BORN, IN NIMES

and statues. The Church of St. Agricol is ancient and was restored in 1321, with later additions. There are several interesting items in the interior.

The Musée Calvet has on its main floor Roman antiquities, Gallic sculptures, several tombs, and the Municipal Library with nearly two hundred thousand books and four thousand manuscripts, some of the latter being of great historic importance. The Picture Gallery has several important canvases, including one by Mme. Vigée Lebrun.

First among the excursions from Avignon, we cross the bridge to Villeneuve. If for no other reason, it is desirable to leave the City of the Popes so as to experience the thrill of returning to it, as its grandeur and dignity increase each step of the way—"Avignon with its tower and belfries all pointing up to the sky—Avignon so filled in ancient days with glory and splendor that she need no longer trouble her head about them." Villeneuve was the residence of prelates and was a thriving place in the days of the Avignon Popes, and there remain many relics of that time. The Church of Notre Dame dates from the early fourteenth century and contains several good pictures. The Hospice, once a convent, contains the tomb of Pope Innocent VI and a small museum. From the Fort St. André we may obtain a fine view of the river, and then arrive at the ruins of the Chartreuse du Val-de-

Bénédiction, founded by Pope Innocent VI in the year 1356.

In less than one hour we may make the excursion to the Fontaine de Vaucluse, immortalized by Petrarch. The spring, which is the source of the Sorgne, is in a circle of rocks and gushes from a cavern when the water is high. Apparently it is fed by a large underground stream, as there is a great volume of water, some of which is used for the driving of mills. Petrarch retired to this spot in 1337.

The next high spot in our journey is Nimes, one of the most interesting of all French towns, if one desires to make a close observation of Roman remains; here they stand out, unhampered, as they are in some places, by constructions of the Middle Ages. This place, which probably was of considerable importance in prehistoric times, submitted to the Romans over a century before the beginning of the Christian

OLD ROMAN ARENA AT NIMES, SO WELL PRESERVED THAT BULL-FIGHTS ARE HELD IN IT

era. It soon became a chief colony, and the conquerors embellished it with temples, theaters, arenas, a forum, and splendid thermæ. It is said that Christianity was taught here in the fourth century.

The first monument to attract our attention is the ancient amphitheater, Les Arènes, which, altho smaller than several others, notably at Rome and Verona, is in a better state of preservation. It is seventy feet high and is built of large blocks of limestone without mortar. Each of the two stories has sixty arches, the lower ones having buttresses and the upper ones Doric columns. As we enter the vast construction, which had seating capacity for twenty thousand persons, we note that its masonry is more than a hundred feet thick. The building dates from the first and second centuries; but it is still in use for bull-fights and athletic games,

THE MAISON CARREE AT NIMES, ONE OF THE FINEST
ROMAN TEMPLES IN THE WORLD

as well as for operatic performances and dramatic spectacles.

Of even greater importance, however, is the so-called Maison Carrée, one of the finest of all Roman temples, a splendid rectangular building with thirty Corinthian columns nearly thirty feet high, fluted and crowned by capitals of exquisite workmanship. From the marks of the metal that held the inscription to the pediment, it is believed that it was erected in the first century and dedicated to Caius and Lucius Cæsar, grandsons of Augustus. It is thought that it stood in the forum, as the foundations of other buildings remain near by. It was carefully restored in 1824 and converted into a museum, which contains some fine antique statues, notably the celebrated Venus of Nimes, vases, medals, and works in bronze, iron and bone.

The so-called Temple of Diana is believed to have been connected with the hot baths, of which there are remains in the neighborhood. The façade has three arcades, and the interior consists of a large hall with stone vaulting and twelve niches for statues. The Cathedral of Notre Dame et St. Castor is said to rest upon the foundations of a temple of Augustus. The façade has a frieze, probably dating from the eleventh century, that has scenes from the Book of Genesis. The interior has a Christian sarcophagus for an altar, a broad Romanesque nave, small chapels at the sides, and several interesting paintings. The Porte d'Auguste is a four-arched gateway of Roman fortifications that date from the age of Augustus. The Museum of Painting and Sculpture is another point of interest that should not be overlooked. Among its gems are: an antique mosaic, Le Brun's "St. John," Jan Steen's "Woman Holding a Glass," Vernet's "Women Bathing," and many works by other painters of more or less note.

THE MAIN STREET OF ARLES—NO OVERCROWDING

Among excursions out of Nimes, I recommend the trips to Uzès, to Ganges, and to Aigues-Mortes. The last-named town has fortifications that are counted among the great architectural curiosities of France; perhaps one might justly say that they are superior to all others, since they are uniform in style and of one date. The walls are twenty-five to thirty-three feet high, and have fifteen towers and ten gates.

At Tarascon we think of Tartarin, the hero of Daudet's satirical romance; also of St. Martha of Bethany, whose tomb is in the church that bears her name, and of King René of Anjou, whose splendid Gothic château is now a prison. Also of the Tarasque, the cruel monster which, according to the legend, ravaged the country during the first century of the Christian era. The celebrated festival of the Tarasque, usually ascribed to René, was revived in 1861 by Mistral and occurs on the Sunday before Ascension, when a procession is formed—led by the Order of the Knights of Tarasque —and goes up the mountain to the statue of Our Lady of the Castle. The people from all the neighboring towns arrive to see the statue taken to the church, where it remains until Ascension, and on Whitsunday there is a great feast. The girls of all the near-by towns show their finery and the men wear fantastic costumes. Everyone attends mass, and then takes place the great procession, in which St. Martha is represented by a beautiful girl dressed in white and wearing a blue veil. She bears a jar of holy water and leads the Tarasque by a silk thread. After the procession, the fun begins and everyone makes merry. Shepherds carry a tableau of the Holy Family, there is a survival of pagan celebrations in the Planting of the Vine ceremony, porters are accompanied by St. Christopher bearing the Child Jesus on his shoulder, and carts decorated with flowers move among the crowds. Sometimes it becomes a hilarious spectacle at the close; but it is much enjoyed by the inhabitants and visitors.

A railway journey of less than an hour brings us to St. Remy, which occupies the site of the once famous Roman town of Glanum Livii. Relics of its ancient day of splendor survive in the fine Triumphal Arch, ornamented with a garland of leaves and fruit, and a mausoleum, known as "The Tomb of the Julii" on account of an inscription. It has three stories and rises to a height of sixty feet. A square base has hunting scenes and battles. There is an arrangement of porticos and fluted half-columns, and surmounting all is a small round temple with ten fluted Corinthian columns, containing two draped statues. Probably the whole edifice dates from the beginning of the Christian era.

How many small towns you visit in this vicinity while

making your leisurely journey down the Rhone will depend very largely upon the time at your disposal. Each large town or small village has something to reward the traveler; but even an enthusiastic and observing visitor to Provence may tire of Roman remains, and, after visiting several of the smaller places in the Rhone district, is likely to pass on to Arles, where the antique relics are upon a huge scale.

Arles, the origin of which is unknown, was a rival of

CLOISTERS OF ST. TROPHIME AT ARLES

Marseilles in the days of Julius Cæsar, and sometimes was called "the Gallic Rome"; it is likely that here we obtain a better view of Roman provincial life than in almost any place in Europe. Here, also, in the present city of about thirty thousand inhabitants, we see some of the most strikingly beautiful girls in France—girls with Greek features and carriage, and with an attractive manner of dressing, as well as of arranging the hair. Constantine frequently resided here and built a large stone bridge. At that time the population was at least three times as much as it is to-day. It is thought that Christianity was taught here by Trophimus, a disciple of St. Paul. The city has a harbor of some importance, altho it is twenty-seven miles from the mouth of the Rhone. Also, it is one of the best cities in which to study the real Provence, to see and know its people, and to attempt to understand them.

It is said that grape-vines and olives were brought here direct from Greece, and flourished. Greek place-names survive to a considerable extent despite the long Roman occupation, and it is likely that the whole neighborhood has much in common with ancient Attica. The Arlesian has a fondness for festivals of all kinds, bull-fights, the native dances, dress and speech. As someone has suggested, Arles was originally a Greek city in the midst of Roman Gaul, and it still has a distinctive spirit.

The Arena, a Roman amphitheater, was built at the beginning of the Christian era and is one of the largest in France; it seats twenty-six thousand spectators, but is not so well preserved as the one at Nimes. It has two stories of sixty arcades. In the eighth century it was converted into a fortress, three towers of which are still in position. Despite its somewhat ruined condition, bull-fights are still held in it during the summer months.

Southwest of the Arena is the splendid Roman Theater, finished in the third century. It was drawn upon in the fifth century—and later—as a quarry for church buildings and other edifices. Originally, however, it is certain that the theater was lavishly embellished, as many fine works of art have been found here, including the celebrated Venus of Arles, now in the Louvre at Paris. Crossing the stage and

ALL THAT IS LEFT OF THE ROMAN THEATER AT ARLES

forming a permanent background was a colonnade, probably representing a temple. Two of the columns remain in position, one of Carrara marble; and the ruins indicate that marble was freely used in covering the surface of the exquisite edifice. Much of the stone from the theater went for the building of the cloisters of the old Cathedral of St. Trophime, which is said to rest upon the foundations of the Roman prætorium. The church is in the Romanesque style; the portal has six columns, which rest upon lions, with statues of the Apostles between them. A sculptured frieze shows Apostles standing between the Elect and the Condemned. The font near the entrance rests on the front of an ancient sarcophagus. There are fine tapestries covering the walls of the interior, and an early Christian sarcophagus serves as an altar.

The Musée Lapidaire, occupying the old Church of Ste. Anne, has a rare collection of antique sarcophagi and other relics of the ancient world, found in the neighborhood. Some of the notable items are: an altar of Apollo (not Leda) decorated with swans, palms and laurels; Roman bugles, glass, bronze; the god Mithras encircled by a snake; a colossal statue of Augustus; a mosaic showing "The Rape of Europa." Fully as interesting as this collection is that in the Museon Arlaten, which was founded by Mistral and installed in 1909 with the aid of his Nobel prize money. Here we find a splendid ethnographical exhibition illustrating Provençal costumes, industries, traditions, customs, and all that is thought to contribute to the national life. The Place du Forum is the site of the ancient Roman forum and is still the center of activities. It has a statue of Mistral. The

VIEW OF ROMAN ARENA AT ARLES, SHOWING ARCH CONSTRUCTION

Palais de Constantine, as it is called to-day, doubtless is a relic of the ancient Thermæ. South of the town is the Aliscamps, once a Roman burial-ground and later consecrated for Christian burial. Like the Valley of Jehoshaphat at Jerusalem, this cemetery acquired great celebrity and bodies were brought to it from great distances for interment. It is mentioned by Dante in his "Inferno." Later, the place became neglected, the monuments were destroyed, and the best of the sarcophagi were removed to the museum and the cathedral.

There are many delightful excursions from Arles to small towns in the region, all of which have points of great interest for the casual visitor or the antiquarian. One who comes this way in spring will enjoy the trip to the Ile de la Camargue, which has an area of about three hundred square miles and lies in the delta of the Rhone. Les Saintes-Maries, a once important town on the coast, owes its name to Mary of Bethany, Mary the mother of James, and Mary Magdalene, who, according to legend, landed here with Martha of Bethany, her risen brother Lazarus who became the first bishop of Marseilles, Sara their black servant, and St. Maximinus. The church was restored by King René and is said to contain the tombs of two of the Marys, while the relics of Sara repose in the crypt. In the center of the church is a fountain, which is said to have burst forth at the time of the arrival of the saints. The church is a popular center of Provençal pilgrimage, the gipsies coming in large numbers to pay homage to Sara.

XV AIX AND MARSEILLES

CHATEAU D'IF, THE ISLAND PRISON MADE FAMOUS BY MONTE CRISTO'S THRILLING ESCAPE

XV

AIX AND MARSEILLES

AIX-EN-PROVENCE was the oldest Roman colony in Gaul, dating from 123 B. C. and owing its name to its thermal waters. To-day there is not much of the town that existed before the barbaric invasions, when it was in its period of splendor, both as a Roman colony and as the capital of Provence. In those days the court at Aix fostered the Provençal language and did much to attract the attention of Europe. It seems always to have been a great favorite with its guests, whether they came for peace or for war. Marius and Julius Cæsar each won a great victory in the neighborhood and both did what they could to beautify the place. Well into the days of the Empire, Aix was beloved of the Roman rulers, and great arenas and theaters were built for the amusement of the people. Situated on the Aurelian Road, it was open to attack, however, and the whole town was destroyed several times by enemy raids; but under Charlemagne it prospered again, and for something like six centuries it was the capital of Provence, which lived independent from France.

It is natural that our first thought, after we arrive at Aix, is of the good King René, whose statue stands looking down the Cours Mirabeau, holding a bunch of grapes. This is not to suggest that he was a disciple of Bacchus, but rather that he did all in his power to encourage grape culture. Critical history gives him a high place as an enlightened monarch and proves that he deserved his title of "the Good King." It is true that he taxed heavily, and he was guilty of massacres; but he endeavored, according to the standards of his time, to be a father to his people. He inaugurated a festival at Aix that was partly religious and partly pagan, at any rate proving that he desired his subjects to make merry; and perhaps he wished to interest the guilds and corporations, which were likely, at times, to become troublesome. The festival at Aix began on Whitmonday and progressed until Corpus Christi. On the former day, the people elected the Prince of Love, the Abbé of Youth, and other dignitaries, including the King of the Gown and Wig. A solemn procession was held the evening before Trinity Sunday, and all the people were apprised of the fact that the great ceremonial would take place the next day. The day was largely given over to visits to dignitaries, and at ten in the evening Fame came riding a horse through the streets with four guides attending.

WHERE SUMMER SUNSHINE IS THE REAL THING:
AIX-EN-PROVENCE

THE HANDSOME "FONTAINE DE LA ROTONDE" IN AIX

Then came the Duke and Duchess of Urbino, followed by Momus and Mercury, and after them came Night.

A group represented the infernal powers, including the Golden Calf of Mount Sinai, with Moses and Aaron; Pluto and Persephone; Herod wearing a crown and carrying a scepter, and several demons attacking him with pitchforks. Then gods and goddesses on horseback; elves, nymphs, the car of Bacchus, the Queen of Sheba, and Solomon; dancers, Venus, Cupid, Laughter, and the Three Fates. The next morning there was a performance of "The Tournament of Armetto," depicting the temptations that attempt to destroy the human soul. All the Guilds were represented and carried their banners, and it seems that the majority of the native population joined the procession. At the end of the festivities, trees were planted.

André Hallays quotes Charles de Brosses as calling Aix "charming throughout, the most charming place in France, after Paris," but Hallays remarks that it has "suffered reverses," adding:

THE COURS MIRABEAU, WITH ITS FINE OLD TREES, IS ONE OF THE ATTRACTIONS OF AIX

"From a capital, it has become a subprefecture; a modest court of appeals has replaced its Parliament; the streets, which were formerly crowded by a multitude of sedan chairs decorated with gold and armorial bearings, are now deserted; there are few strollers under the trees of the courtyards; the only sound which breaks the solemn silence of the public places, is that of fountains. But the external beauty of the past has not disappeared, and the superb façades of the old mansions still testify to the magnificence of former days. To-day Aix is no longer the most charming city of France, for there is too much sadness in the decline of a great city; but as it still possesses its architecture, its statues, and its books, it remains a place without an equal for reverie and leisured labor. Here we breathe the most subtle air which exists in France, for it is the air of Provence; but the very melancholy of things inclines one here to serious thought; here one may experience the exultation of full sunlight and the stinging whip of the mistral, without losing the faculty of reflection; everything here forbids the tumultuous laziness of the people of Marseilles."

Aix is a city of fountains. They greet the visitor on every hand, splashing and trickling jets of water from the ancient aqueducts of Marius the Conqueror. The people seem to have done all in their power to preserve the ancient mansions. The paintings and the carvings have been scattered and now repose in the homes of millionaires in Paris, London, and New York, but some of the most beautiful of the fountains remain—those in public places, as well as those in the vesti-bules of private houses. The Musée contains a collection of pictures, sculptures and antiquities and deserves a visit, if but for a glance at some of its treasures.

There are several churches, but the one that must not be

VIEW OF MARSEILLES AND THE CHATEAU D'IF FROM NOTRE DAME DE LA GARDE

overlooked is the Cathedral of the Holy Saviour, which had an early origin, but which in its present form dates from the eleventh century. The octagonal Baptistry is said to occupy the site of a Temple of Apollo. It has eight antique columns, six of them of green marble, and the Seven Sacraments, paintings by Aix artists. In the choir is a Flemish tapestry of the sixteenth century, with scenes from the life of Jesus and the Virgin, originally destined for Canterbury Cathedral. The Chapel of St. Mitre has the fifth-century sarcophagus of the saint and his miracle on wood. On the high altar is "The Raising of Lazarus." The Library has nearly two hundred thousand volumes and thirteen hundred manuscripts, including King René's "Book of Hours," illuminated by himself, and a missal of 1422.

Méry said: "Si Paris avait une Cannebière, ce serait un petit Marseille." We recall this humorous quip when we arrive in the chief port of the Mediterranean, a city that is not in great favor with American tourists, but should be visited by them, not because it is a convenient point of departure for the coast of North Africa, but because it is one of the most interesting of cities, too often overlooked by travelers. For Marseilles, like Cairo, seems to be a melting-pot of the nations, and there is such an unusual population in few cities of the earth. Do you remember Dickens's vivid description of Marseilles and its strange mixture of races under the midsummer sun—in the first chapter of "Little Dorrit"? In the streets of this southern cosmopolis we meet Greek, Jew, Lascar, Arab, Maltese, Catalan, Portuguese, and Provençal, as well as Marseillais; white and black and brown, many of them in distinctive costumes. Francis Miltoun has written:

"The Marseillais *pur sang* (except that it has been many

SHIPPING IN THE OLD HARBOR OF MARSEILLES

centuries since he has been *pur sang*) is a unique type among the inhabitants of France, the product of many successive immigrations from most of the Mediterranean countries. He is indeed an extraordinary development, tho in no way outré or unsympathetic, in spite of being a bloodthirsty-looking individual. To describe him were impossible. The Marseillais is a Marseillais by his dark complexion, by his svelt figure, and by the exuberance of his gestures and his voice. Always ready for adventure, or pleasure, he is the very stuff of another day, of which the sea-rovers were made."

Marseilles has been called a southern Babylon. It is one of the gayest cities in the world, as anyone will appreciate who makes a tour of the Cannebière, a principal thorough-fare, which lives up to its reputation for worldliness. Some-times it has seemed to me that this street is the very symbol of the city. It has many fine avenues, some of which, altho not so crowded, seem as interesting as the boulevards of Paris; but the Cannebière is Marseilles, the heart of the second city of France. It has been said that the remainder of this city is asleep by ten o'clock (which is not literally true), but the Cannebière throws on its full lights at that hour and the hilarity continues until two o'clock in the morning. This is Marseilles, which, unlike the other cities of antiquity, has progressed, improved, and developed for something like twenty-five centuries. It was founded about six hundred years before the dawn of the Christian era, upon the site of a still earlier settlement; and long before Jesus taught on the Sea of Galilee, it had attained grandeur and opulence. Many similar cities of the antique world have faded to insignificance or entirely passed out of existence and almost from memory, but Marseilles has added to its glory with the

MARSEILLES SEEN ACROSS THE "BASSIN DE CARENAGE"

passing of the centuries. It is a survival of Greek, Roman, Frankish, and feudal civilization; but it is a grand survival, and to-day is more illustrious than during any period of its proud history.

Founded by Phocæans from Asia Minor, the city was occupied by Carthaginians in 535 B. C., but recaptured. The Massilians, as they were then called, were recognized as masters of the sea; they founded new colonies along the

FORT ST. JEAN, AT THE ENTRANCE TO THE
OLD HARBOR, MARSEILLES

Mediterranean coast, and even explored the shores of western Africa and northern Europe. The city invoked the aid of Rome against hostile tribes, and remained independent until beseiged by Julius Cæsar in 49 B. C. Christianity was introduced in the third century by St. Victor, and the city had famous schools. It is even asserted that Lazarus, after he arose from the tomb, fled hither from Palestine and became the first bishop; to support that claim, however, there is only legend and not historical certainty. Marseilles has had a remarkable history down through the ages; but the feature

[316]

of it all is that the city sur-
vives, and that events such as
the conquest of Algiers and
the building of the Suez Canal
have added to its importance.
To-day, it is in direct steamship communication with all
the world. It remains the chief
port of the Mediterranean. It
is the center of the soap industry, being situated in the
midst of olive culture, which
provides not only the olive oil
of commerce, but the best of
soaps, including the cele-

OBELISK, CASTELLANE SQUARE,
MARSEILLES

brated kind so long known to our mothers as Castile soap.

The fishing industry seems always to have been important,
as the ancient government guaranteed certain privileges,
which were confirmed by later rulers—Louis XI, Francis I,
Henry II, Henry IV. Desiring to outdo his predecessors,
Louis XIII granted to Marseilles a special price on salt. Fishing rights and powers were extended to the "Prud'hommes
de Marseille," who formed a sort of court, which regulated
all disputes between members. These officials still exist, but
unfortunately their picturesque costume has disappeared, and
one no longer sees them in the street with the Henri IV
mantle, a toque for a hat, and a two-handed sword.

Marseilles has undergone a marvelous topographical trans-
formation in recent times. It was one of the first cities in
France to cut great thoroughfares through old sections where
there were narrow, circling streets, and one of the first to
erect fine modern palaces for the transaction of civic busi-

ness. The Rue de la République is one of the boulevards produced in this fashion, and while it still shows certain structures that are inferior, it is one of the world's great streets and is a joy to all who see it for the first time. Marseilles is sumptuous in appearance; we soon realize that, in general exterior indications it is in lively comparison with the heart of Paris itself. The author of "Rambles on the Riviera" remarks that "La société Marseillaise is no less endowed with good taste and the love of luxurious appointments and surroundings than is the most Parisian of Parisian circles—a term which has come to mean much in the refinements of modern life."

The Vieux-Port first attracts our attention—the Lakydon of the Phocæans—a basin of seventy acres, now used by smaller craft, but one of the interesting scenes of southern Europe. It has been called "a museum of the old marine but for the great ocean-going yachts at anchor." Most of the boats seen here are "lateen-rigged, piratical-looking craft, which, regardless of the fact that they are evidently best suited for the seafaring of these parts, invariably give the stranger the idea that they are something of an exotic nature which has come down to us through the makers of school histories. They are as strange-looking to-day as would be the caravels of Columbus or the Viking ships of the Northmen." Here we see all types of small Mediterranean craft, most of them with a narrow prow ornamented with the conventional figure of the olden days. The sailors on these boats, hailing as they do from a hundred ports, add to the picturesque scene ashore; and while tourists are warned that it is not always safe to prowl about the cafés and places where they congregate for their pleasure, they should be seen, because they make an important contribution to the cosmo-

CHURCH OF NOTRE DAME DE LA GARDE, MARSEILLES

politan aspect that is the real picture of historic Marseilles.

Towering far above the city is the notable Church of Notre Dame de la Garde, on the fortified summit of the hill south of the harbor. Naturally, it is a church of pilgrimage and one beloved by the seagoing folk, who bid land goodby, as they sail forth, with their eyes upon the Virgin on the tower that seems to stand guarding the whole sea, and who look up to her when they return, and see her standing almost in the clouds as the buildings of the waterfront slowly come nearer and nearer. One goes up the hill by lift, or, more piously, makes the ascent on foot. There are one hundred and forty steps to the lower church; one hundred and seventy-four to the upper. The sanctuary of the Middle Ages has been replaced by a large edifice in neo-Byzantine style, over the façade of which is a colossal statue of the Virgin by Lequesne. The interior of the church is brilliant

with mosaics, and on the high altar is a silver figure of the
Virgin in the crypt. One may ascend the tower and obtain
a splendid view of the city and harbor, for here, despite the
smoke of steamers, the sky and the water are blue, the sun
shines, and one sees plainly great distances away.

The Cathedral, known as Marie-Majeure, stands on a terrace near the beginning of the New Harbor. It is in

A PRIVATE CONFERENCE ON AFFAIRS OF STATE

Romanesque-Byzantine style, is four hundred sixty feet long,
and was erected in the last century of green and white stone.
Here are marbles and mosaics in keeping with the brilliant
colors to be observed elsewhere in the region.

The Musée des Beaux-Arts should be visited, as it contains
much of interest. On the ground floor we find: modern
French sculpture, a room entirely devoted to the works of
Pierre Puget of Marseilles, a cabinet containing frescoes and

drawings attributed to Correggio, and a cabinet of water-colors and engravings. The
staircase has mural paintings,
"Marseilles as a Greek Colony" and "The Gate of the
East" by Puvis de Chavannes.
The central room on the first
floor has many first-class
paintings, notably portraits
by Greuze, Duplessis, Mi-
gnard, "Fête Champêtre" by
Watteau, Tintoretto's "The
Doge Morosini," Paolo Veronese's "Venetian Princess,"
sketches by Rubens, Perugi-

FRANCE ALSO HAS HER WILD
INDIANS

no's "Family of the Virgin," and a tavern scene by Ribera.
The room to the left of the entrance has works by modern
artists, notably: Corot's "Southern Tyrol," Courbet's "Stag
Drinking," Regnault's "Judith and Holofernes," a classical
hunting-scene by Puvis de Chavannes, and Millet's "Mother
and Child."

There are several splendid buildings, fine promenades and
avenues; but Marseilles is a city to be visited with no particular itinerary or schedule. One should wander about with
his eyes open, and always with the assurance that he will
come upon scenes and characters that are unusual if he hails
from the lands of grayer skies. A pretty excursion takes
one to the park, where the Archeological Museum is housed
in the Château Borély, near to which is the Botanical Garden.
The race-course is near the seashore, and there are numerous
cafés and restaurants in the vicinity. The Bourse is a splen-

ISLAND OF CHATEAU D'IF AND ITS CASTLE-PRISON
OF THE SAME NAME

did edifice; so is the Palais de Justice, the vestibule of which
has relief figures of famous legislators. The Church of St.
Victor once belonged to the abbey of the same name that
was founded in the fifth century by St. Cassian and rebuilt
several times, once by Pope Urban V, who had been its abbot.
The crypt contains a "Grotto of St. Lazarus," a Virgin of
the fourth century, a cross said to have been that upon
which St. Andrew was martyred, and ancient tombs. The
Triumphal Arch in the Place d'Aix was erected 1825-32 to
commemorate a victory near Cadiz. The Palais de Long-
champ is a splendid Renaissance-style building, in the center
of which is a triumphal arch, connected by columns with
large side-buildings. In front is a cascade over a flight of
steps and a basin which has a large sculptured group.

The Corniche Road begins beyond the fort and follows
the coast toward Nice and Monte Carlo. This road, which is
most agreeable when the weather is not too warm, is cut
from solid rock in many places and affords another beautiful
view of the harbor. One may take this route to meet the

[322]

Prado, which is a popular promenade and much in vogue as evening approaches. The Prado is two miles long, and many villas may be observed along the way. The people of Marseilles are unusually proud of their country homes. Some of these are large and sumptuously furnished, and ornamented by splendid gardens; the smaller ones, too, are very attractive, being picturesquely set in canyons and hillsides that overlook the sea.

American tourists are always particularly interested in the excursion from the Old Port to the famous Château d'If on the island of the same name, a ride by boat of about two miles. The castle was immortalized by Alexandre Dumas in "Monte Cristo," and his excellent word-picture of it in that great romance has made it familiar to all the world. It is a keep built in 1529 and has been used as a state prison. Its

A GLIMPSE OF TOULON IN LIBERTY SQUARE

principal dungeons are viewed by the visitor, and the stories of the guides as to "exact locations" may be accepted or rejected, according to individual taste.

If we happen to be going toward Hyères and the Riviera, we may find it worth while to pause at the neighboring Mediterranean city, Toulon, and see its fine harbor. With the exception of Brest, Toulon is the most important coast fortress and naval station in France. The large arsenal here cannot be visited by foreigners without a great deal of signing and countersigning of official papers; but the visitor will find the twelfth-century Church of Ste. Marie-Majeure and the Musée-Bibliothèque of considerable interest. It was in the siege of Toulon, you may remember, that an artillery officer named Napoleon Bonaparte first distinguished himself in 1793 by driving out the Royalists who were trying to crush the Revolution.

XVI RIVIERA TOWNS

VISTA OF NICE SHOWING AT A GLANCE WHY IT IS EUROPE'S FAVORITE WINTER RESORT

XVI

RIVIERA TOWNS

WHO does not thrill at the mention of any of the beautiful Mediterranean towns scattered along the coast east of Marseilles! Even their names fall pleasantly on the ears. One who has visited them is even more enthusiastic in anticipation of a return visit than one who looks forward to seeing them for the first time. In the recollections and anticipations of everyone, they evoke pictures of flowers, fragrance, sunshine, sea and sky that seem never so azure or sapphire elsewhere. And this is only one of the vivid landscape colors, which also include ocher, myrtle-green, purple, flaming red! They are in the picture as one views the hills from the seashore; and never elsewhere do villas seem quite so beautifully situated. Predominantly white, these villas also take on the colors of the rainbow as they perch upon cliffs overlooking scenes that the artists of the world attempt to paint for the delectation of theater audiences. Here they are in nature—thousands of views that would bring applause and astonishment, perhaps unbelief, if they appeared upon canvas.

The French Riviera has prompted admiration for over two thousand years, and the number of zealous devotees increases each year. Its fame as a refuge from ice and snow has been known to Europeans for many centuries, and now Americans also seem to have learned that these Mediterranean towns are delightful retreats during the summer months.

A MORNING WALK

The golden sunshine here can be quite warm in the middle of the day, so that one may prefer not to indulge in strenuous exercises; but these Riviera towns are also delightful places of residence, if one learns a lesson from the natives and lives as they do. There are refreshing breezes at night. One awakens to behold a panorama of beauty hitherto unsuspected. Perhaps it is not a place for work; but it is an ideal locality for recreation and rest. The whole French Mediterranean coast also has acquired a summertime vogue with Americans that was undreamed of a generation ago.

Let us assume that we have crossed from Italy, or that we have come directly from the north to Nice, which is the capital of the Maritime Alps. Nice is a city of nearly one hundred thousand inhabitants, and altho it has a history reaching back to ancient times, it is appreciated by visitors not so much for its past as for its present. It was founded by inhabitants of Marseilles in the fourth century B. C., and was known to the ancient Greeks as Nicæa. It had a tragic history in the early days; but it survived, and to-day is more popular and prosperous than ever.

Nice has its Old Town with narrow streets, and its Strangers' Quarters, which is larger than the original town. It has been said that "you have to give Nice time, and get out of your rut, before you awaken to its unique charac-

GENERAL VIEW OF THE RIVIERA NEAR NICE

NICE ALSO HAS ITS BUSY HARBOR

teristics." Then if you detach yourself from the amuse-
ment-seekers, the time-killers, the apathetic, the bored, the
blasé, and the conscientious tourists, you begin to realize
that "the metropolis of the Riviera (including its suburbs
and Monte Carlo) is a world in itself—an inexhaustible
reservoir for exploration and reflection." Americans
(North and South) say that they feel at home in Nice,
because it was made by and for everybody and caters to
everyone.

A million pleasure-seekers now go to Nice every year
from a score of different countries. A place that holds
such enchantment must have the solid attractions of one of
the pleasure-grounds of the world. Nice itself is delightful,
and many travelers prefer to remain there all through the
season; but it is also a city that can be used as a base for

ON THE PALM-FRINGED PROMENADE AT NICE

many excursions to surrounding towns, the extent of the sojourn depending upon one's leisure. There is a climate that appeals particularly to invalids, as the locality is sheltered by the Maritime Alps, which make the average temperature higher than that of Paris in winter and lower in summer; in fact, the temperature is considered more comfortable for elderly persons and for convalescents than that of any other point along the coast.

GROTTO IN THE PUBLIC GARDEN AT NICE

We do not visit Nice for the routine sights that we would expect to find in other towns; nevertheless, it has several local attractions, such as the Municipal Museum; the Casino, with a winter garden, gambling rooms, and a theater; the Jardin Public; the pretty Promenade des Anglais, shaded by palms and having a number of sumptuous hotels; the harbor and the Quai du Midi, a prolongation of the Promenade; also the Opera and the Public Library. For the visitor whose interests go beyond the society of the Prome-

TOURING ON THE CORNICHE D'OR

nade and its hotels, the city offers relics of other days, altho one must search for them; they do not stand forth as do the arenas, theaters, and arches of some of the other cities. The streets are crooked and narrow, down around the Old Port, and the children are noisy. For one who enjoys the associations of historical spots, however, there are several buildings—now in partial decay and surrounded by evidences of poverty—that once knew the laughter of noble ladies and knights, and looked down upon processions of famous prelates.

There is the Lascaris Palace, for example, in the narrow Rue Droite; it is named for the great family of Theodore Lascaris, who, driven from his Byzantine throne in the thirteenth century, found a refuge at Nice. There remain windows, stairways and frescoes that are reminiscent of the glorious days. The old market is built upon the foundations of the ancient wall, and one who is imaginative can easily conjure up scenes that took place here during the invasions of the Saracens. A single tower is all that remains of the ancient château. Near here, landed Jeanne, the Queen of Naples, who left a reputation similar to that of Cleopatra, Queen of Egypt. What is now the flower market was once the center of fashion at Nice, when belles in crinoline skirts and their beaux clad in satin met for the promenade, then deemed as important as a stroll upon the

Promenade des Anglais to-day. Where the marble cross now stands was the Convent of the Holy Cross, notable in history for the meeting of Pope Paul III, King Francis I, and the Emperor Charles V, each of whom arrived in state, surrounded by a resplendent retinue.

Nice upon the hillside has watched the centuries glide by, as the Sphinx of Egypt has seen nations rise and fall. The harbor has witnessed the purple sails of Roman galleys and the long marine procession down through the ages to the great liners that now bring thousands of visitors for a holiday. Where the latest dance of to-day is in vogue, there were dancing maidens paying tribute to ancient gods and goddesses. Where Roman trumpets sounded the triumph, American negro bands now play jazz music. That is Nice—eternally beautiful and always attracting the homage of Dame Fashion's devotees and the admiration of the world.

We motor from Nice to Mentone by the Route de la Corniche, which was built by Napoleon I and is highly preferable to the railway journey. As we ascend the hills on this famous drive, a splendid vegetation constantly attracts our attention, and there are superb views of Nice and its surroundings. Many towns attract us along the way; but we shall make various excursions in the district, visiting them later, so let us go first to Monaco, the capital of

OCEANOGRAPHIC MUSEUM, MONACO

MONTE CARLO AND HARBOR ENTRANCE SEEN FROM MONACO

the principality of the same name. The town consists of the old part, on a picturesque promontory, and the new section on the bay below. The new section is now a fashionable health resort in winter and a favorite bathing-place in summer. The name is derived from a temple of Herakles Monoikos, and Hercules is the mythical founder. The Cathedral is dedicated to St. Nicholas, sometimes considered the successor to Neptune; so in the past, as at present, Monaco has loved the sea. Here is a great Marine Museum, where one sees a splendid collection of sea monsters in their natural surroundings, and learns of the manner in which they were caught. Princes of Monaco have long been worshipers of the sea and its mysteries, and have left many souvenirs of their voyages. The Anthropological Museum contains the ancient skeletons unearthed at Garavan, third-century jewelry, and tombs of Roman Christians with the bones inside. The Palace is the chief sight, as it is beautifully furnished and enjoys a magnificent location and view. The large garden is open to visitors.

It is a little more than a mile from Monaco to Monte Carlo, famous for its mild climate, its beauty, and its gambling. When we arrive, we go at once to see the Casino, which sits on a promontory east of the town and has given rise to fantastic stories that have stirred the imagination of the world. This building is the symbol of man's weakness for gaming—also of Monaco's freedom from taxation and military service. Everyone must show his passport and pay a fee before he is permitted to enter the Casino. The blanched faces of the players, the excitement and evident nervous strain, intrigue the onlooker, and one hears ghastly tales of suicides due to the loss of fortunes. There is a variety of opinion concerning the institution;

[335]

MONACO PROPER, ON ITS BOLD HEADLAND, WITH THE OLD PALACE IN THE FOREGROUND

but it should be recalled always that there is no law compelling people to risk their money at the tables. The games played at the Casino are roulette and trente-et-quarante. In roulette there are thirty-six numbers and a zero, upon any one of which the player can stake his money. If he is successful, he receives from the Bank thirty-five times as much as he risked. There are various regulations in favor of the Bank in both games. In front of the Casino are fine gardens in which there are exotic and subtropical trees and shrubs; and behind it is a terrace upon which trap-shooting attracts the best shots of all countries. The Promenade along the sea at Monte Carlo is the most fashionable and beautiful on the French Riviera.

It takes about twenty minutes to go by mountain railway up to La Turbie, rising thirteen hundred feet in the two-mile trip. It is an ancient village, visited by tourists primarily for the excellent view; but it also has great historical importance, altho its monuments are in ruins. It contains the fallen stones of the Trophy of Augustus, erected more than nineteen centuries ago in honor of the Emperor who not far away gained a victory over the Ligurians. The Roman Senate decreed the building of this fine monument, which was meant to proclaim to the world the superiority of Rome and the glory of the Roman Empire. Several classical writers refer to it, and a close study of all of them seems to show that this memorial was over two hundred feet in height, and built of marble and polished granite. The four sides measured over two hundred feet each, and a plinth arose from these upon which rested a Doric colonnade. In the center was a Doric tower about one hundred feet in circumference, with eleven pillars supporting it. The names of conquered tribes were engraved upon it, and statues of the

PAUSING FOR A REST ALONG THE PROMENADE AT MONTE CARLO

BEAUTY HAUNTS MONTE CARLO EVEN ON ITS WHARVES

generals, officials, and commanders of the army in this region were in niches, with the gigantic statue of the Emperor crowning all.

It has been described as "one of the greatest monuments which the Romans ever raised, and now fallen, like the power which built it." This seemingly unimportant place was once the Acropolis of Monaco, and its foundation dates

WHERE MILLIONS ARE LOST AND WON:
THE CASINO, MONTE CARLO

back to the Phenicians. Probably the Trophy of Augustus occupies the site of a Phenician Temple to Hercules, and the Christian church is built from the stones of the Roman monument. About half a mile from La Turbie is Laghet, a favorite resort of pilgrims; it is a dependency of a convent founded in the seventeenth century. The miraculous statue of the Virgin stands in a niche surrounded by votive offerings, and the cloisters are hung with pictures recording the miracles. Giacinta Porta, wife of Casanova of Monaco, was

ENTERING THE CASINO AT
MONTE CARLO

healed here of leprosy in 1652, and it is recorded that within one year the place was visited by over fifty processions, each containing five hundred to five thousand persons.

On the top of a hill, reached by the road from La Turbie to Beaulieu, is the little town of Eze, which may have been a commercial center in the days of the Phenicians. It is certain that the Romans had a station at this place. In the early days of the Christian era a stronghold of some kind stood here, and in the sixth century a castle was built to look out over that cliff to the sea. Life is still quaint and picturesque in Eze: women filling their water-jars and raising them to their heads for the journey homeward, as they stop to visit with friends; men who have little in common with the social world on the seashore. Here dwelt Blacas, the troubadour, some of whose songs have come down to us, and of whom it was said: "He was beloved by his friends and dreaded by his enemies."

We feel that we are approaching the climax of a beautiful drama. The Grande Corniche descends and joins the Petite Corniche at Cap Martin, and not far away the Promenade du Midi brings us to Mentone. The vegetation seems more tropical, the skies are brighter, and as we draw nearer to it the water seems a more beautiful blue. It has been said that one who has passed over the Promenade du Midi has seen another world, apart from the rest of the French Riviera.

There is a cherished legend of Mentone that will bear repetition. When Adam and Eve were expelled from the Garden of Eden, the wife, woman-like, took a bough of lemons, saying that these would remind them of their old home, "and besides, prove refreshing during our journey." They traveled far, and for one reason and another were not satisfied with the lands through which they passed. Finally, all the lemons but one had been eaten. "I shall keep that," said Eve, "and plant it beside our door when we settle down." Then they reached this great promontory that reaches out into the Mediterranean, and Eve stopped. "Look!" she said to Adam; "we have found it—our second Paradise."

The inhabitants and many visitors declare that while a long time has passed since then, and there have been the

CASINO OF MONTE CARLO: THE SIDE FACING THE SEA

MENTONE NESTLES BETWEEN THE ALPS AND MEDITERRANEAN

WHERE THE ALPS LOOM BEHIND MENTONE HARBOR

inevitable changes, Mentone is still a Paradise. The town is small—about ten thousand inhabitants—but the place is seemingly a bower of lemon and orange trees, carobs, figs, and olives. It is quieter than Cannes or Nice, but its climate is as favorable. There are not many sights, but the Riviera visitor is unlikely to find any spot in the whole region that gives him greater satisfaction. New Mentone has little to do with Old Mentone. The former believes that the latter speaks an unintelligible *patois;* but the dialect of Old Mentone is said to be the colloquial Latin of the Romans, blended with that of races with whom they came in contact. Otho built a castle near here and called it Mons Othonis, which in time became Monthonis, Monthon, Mentoni, and finally Mentone, or, as the French spell it, Menton.

Not many of the palaces of the great past remain, and

IN THE PUBLIC GARDENS AT MENTONE

when we do come upon one, we are likely to see the family washing in the courtyard instead of the rich brocades and gonfalons of powerful lords and ladies. The Cathedral of St. Michel, on a platform, overlooks the sea. On one side of Cathedral Square is the Church of the White Penitents, and down a steep staircase that of the Black Penitents. In the olden days, funerals of the Mentonese were preceded by a company of one or the other, dressed in a costume somewhat like that worn by the brothers of the Misericordia in Florence. Mentone also has its casino, now a rival of Monte Carlo.

XVII   FROM CHAMONIX TO CANNES

ALONG THE "ROUTE DES ALPES" GOING UP TO CHAMONIX

XVII

FROM CHAMONIX TO CANNES

AFTER visiting the eastern towns of the south coast of France, we return to Nice and make it our base for various excursions in other directions. There are many delightful places that easily hold our attention for hours or for days, and it is both comfortable and convenient to return to the Riviera metropolis as a base, always with the anticipation of another interesting jaunt.

Thus a run of only thirty-six miles by railway takes us to the picturesque village of Puget-Théniers, with its ruined château and remains of old ramparts now laid out as gardens. From there a motor-bus ride through the upper valley of the Var takes us to the Gorges of Daluis, whose curious green and red rocks are viewed from a road that runs more than six hundred and fifty feet above the river.

The most magnificent scenery in France is to be found in this eastern part of the Republic. I would highly recommend the journey north from Nice by way of the Route des Alpes. This wonderful highway is one of the most beautiful in Europe, taking the motorist through gorges which at times are so narrow that two cars have difficulty in passing. Here and there the road is cut out of the rock, and one travels over a mere shelf. Occasionally the car runs along the brink of a precipice from which there is a sheer drop of four or five thousand feet.

At times the rocky sides of a gorge tower above one's head

to dizzy heights, and the colors of the shale rock seem to change as they are touched by the rays of the sun. From maroon to golden brown and at times a pinkish hue, the colors vary as the day passes. We stop for the night at Barcellonette, where there are hotel accommodations for the usual crowd of tourists. The following day brings us in sight of the snow-covered Alps with inspiring tho distant views of Mont Blanc. Alpine huts and villas dot the mountain-sides; peasants appear on the steep slopes, farming where a foothold seems impossible. Toward evening on the second day we arrive at Chamonix, which for scenic grandeur is unsurpassed in France.

Chamonix deserves several days if one can spare the time. There are glorious excursions by mountain railway to the Mer de Glace, where one may enjoy the novelty of crossing a

MONT BLANC SEEN FROM CHAMONIX ON A SUMMER DAY

A RIVER OF ICE: THE GLACIER, "MER DE GLACE," IN THE
ALPS NEAR CHAMONIX

real glacier. Accompanied by a guide there is no danger, but
one should not attempt to cross the Mer de Glace without a
guide, as there are crevasses into which one might slip, with
the possibility of a serious, even fatal accident.

We may cross to the Mauvais Pas and descend from there
on foot, or we may return to the railway station by retracing
our steps across the glacier, which for the average tourist is
the less fatiguing. It is now possible to go part way to the
top of the Aiguille du Midi by a cable aerial railway. This
is the first stage of the route followed by climbers intending
to make the difficult ascent of Mont Blanc; but eight or ten
hours of hard and dangerous climbing still remain between
them and the icy summit.

Chamonix affords a climax to a tour of France. It fur-
nishes a thrill even after one has marveled at the magnifi-

CHARMING CHAMONIX, NESTLING HIGH IN THE ALPS

cence of the châteaux, and enjoyed the quaint beauty of
Normandy and Brittany. Inspired by the splendor of the
church buildings, intrigued by the art of the country, one
may find rest and recreation at the resorts; but for the most
lasting impression which nature provides in the French Republic one must go to the mountains, and among all the
beauties there to be found, it is the Alpine village of Chamonix that lingers longest in one's memory.

Let us next go from Nice to Grasse, the city of flowers
and perfume. Not alone is Grasse a place with pretty gardens where roses flourish and where orange blossoms scent
the air, as in Southern California; it is a place where flowers
are grown for their fragrant petals as wheat and rye are
cultivated for bread on an American farm. Over sixty
thousand acres around Grasse are devoted to flowers, yielding
nearly two and one-half million pounds of roses and four
million pounds of orange blossoms each year. We detect the
odor of this vast flower-garden long before we arrive at the
town itself; faintly at first, like the distant odor of a drop
of the perfume that is the chief industrial product of the
place, then more strongly, and finally the air seems laden
with the scent and the ground seems to be covered with
brilliant rugs.

Grasse is so old that its certain history is lost in antiquity.
One story is that it was first settled by a company of Sar-
dinian Jews about six centuries after the dawn of the Christian era. They called their new home Gratia (Grace) and
there are ancient documents with that spelling. The town
was ravaged several times by the Saracens and later by Bar-
bary pirates; but even when it was razed to the ground, it
always arose again. Men were unwilling to let such a beauty
spot remain untenanted. Napoleon visited Grasse at the time

IN THE FOOTHILLS OF THE FRENCH ALPS: MONT BLANC
IN THE DISTANCE

of his escape from Elba. He rode up through the valley
from the shore near Cannes, accompanied by some of his
soldiers and officers. The inhabitants of the town were
thrown into a panic, word having reached them that pirates
were about to attack the place. They barricaded their doorways, and when Bonaparte arrived he found the streets
empty, and went on through toward Castellane. On a
small hill (the place is marked to-day by black cypresses)
he paused for breakfast, and when the people of Grasse
became aware of the identity of their visitor, they attempted
to shower favors upon him.

The people of Grasse think more of the prosperous present
than of the golden past—more of their flowers and perfume
distilleries than of their great moments in history. To glance
into one of these factories, where flowers are piled in hillocks

[352]

like grain in an American mill, is an experience to be remembered. A fat is spread on trays and the blossoms are placed on this. Then the trays are piled upon each other until they reach almost to the ceiling, and are left thus for about twenty-four hours; but every day they are taken down, the faded flowers are removed, and a fresh layer of flowers is spread over the fat. The process is continued for several weeks, until the fat has become impregnated with the perfume of the flowers, after which it is placed in air-tight receptacles with spirits which extract the scent. As in factories that produce a less exotic product than perfume, nothing goes to waste; an inferior article is made from the faded petals, and even the fat is treated with alcohol in a second process and made to produce a scent that can be used in ointments and soap. There are other processes for the manufac-

A CLOSE-UP OF THE CHASMS IN THE MER DE GLACE

[353]

GRASSE, WHERE CARLOADS OF FINE FRENCH PERFUMES ARE MADE

A PERFUME FACTORY AT GRASSE

ture of finer grades of perfume. The rose, violet and lilac, for example, are sometimes simmered in hot fat to extract their essence. Another method is distillation, by which the odor of orange-blossom, lavender, thyme and peppermint is captured and retained. We take greater interest, however, in the flowers themselves; and if we are fortunate enough to arrive at Grasse in May or June, we shall see the pretty pic-

SHOW-ROOM OF A PERFUME FACTORY

ture of women and girls in the huge flower-fields plucking basketfuls of petals from roses and other plants.

Mass on Sunday in the Cathedral is still the chief event of the week at Grasse. Bells sound an early call in this city of flowers, and the people soon begin to congregate beneath the trees before the church. The social hours here are the ones most enjoyed by the populace, which assembles with a holy purpose and then improves the opportunity for visiting. The church is an attractive building with pillars in the nave

STREET FOUNTAIN IN VENCE

and several good pictures. It dates from the thirteenth century, when the bishopric was moved from Antibes, owing to the visits of pirates and the plague, both of which were then all too common in Mediterranean ports.

Below the Corso an iron gate leads to the courtyard of an old mansion, in which there is a fountain and a garden. In this house Fragonard, the celebrated painter, was the guest of his cousin, to whom he sold "works of painting" for thirty-five hundred livres. Among them were four famous panels which he had painted for Madame Du Barry, and which she had rejected. These panels formerly attracted the attention of all visitors to Grasse, who used to beg for the privilege of seeing them. Now the masterpieces are gone, and copies replace them; only sketches by Fragonard remain. Facing the house, on the other side of the road, is a small public garden, which the town has dedicated to the painter. His bust is upon a lofty column, and the setting is distinctly in his own style—pines, cedars and a stone basin. Fragonard was born at Grasse, and his boyhood was spent there. His father suffered a reverse of fortune, and the budding artist was sent to Paris, probably when he was about fourteen years of age. He went to Italy when he was twenty-five, and studied and copied the masters. He did not return to Grasse until his maturity, and then remained but one year.

We take an electric tram from Grasse to Le Bar, a town that grew up around a castle belonging to the Lords of Grasse. The castle remains, but its glory has departed. It has become an inn, where the peasants drink, smoke, and play cards in rooms once graced by the feasts of nobles. The church of the older day remains, and we obtain a fine view of the district from behind it.

The town of Vence stands upon a promontory nearly one thousand feet above the sea. Its only important building is the Cathedral, and its only treasures are a few fragments of Roman sculpture. It is said that the church stands upon the site of an ancient Roman temple to Mars and Cybele, and in the chapel of St. Veran is a sarcophagus, used as an altar, in which the saint was buried. While we are in his church, we recall Antoine Godeau, who was bishop of Vence

TYPICAL OF THE RIVIERA: A HOTEL AT CANNES

[357]

STATUE OF KING EDWARD VII
AT CANNES

and Grasse, but who is better known as the first member of the French Academy.

By motor we go to Castellane, which has a tremendous rock as its background —a rock said to have been revered as a divinity by the early tribes who inhabited the region. It was a place of pilgrimage, where people came to offer sacrifices. They were the Saliniens, who had some remarkable laws and practises, and who punished idleness as the worst of vices. If it was observed that any-

one, no matter of what rank, was becoming stout, his waist was solemnly encircled by the tribe's standard belt— measuring the traditional circumference of a man—and if he was found to exceed the limit, he was beaten, his work was increased, and his food was restricted. These people ate only one meal a day, and that at sunset. According to Strabo, the historian, they slept upon the ground, on a bed of dry leaves or straw.

A CONTENTED SOJOURNER AT
CANNES

Up there on the summit is Our Lady of the Rock. All newly married couples in Castellane must make the pilgrimage to her before the wedding breakfast, or they will have misfortune in their married life. This is only one of many superstitions and quaint customs that are certain to be of great interest to the visitor who stays long enough to discover them.

Cannes, now a very fashionable resort, derived its name from the canes and bamboos which grow plentifully in the

A HOTEL OVERLOOKING THE SEA AT CANNES

neighborhood and are used extensively as vine supports. Unlike most of the places in the vicinity, it is unable to boast of a notable past, but owes its present popularity to Lord Brougham. That Englishman, we are told, was halted here by a cholera epidemic that had broken out in Italy, and, being in search of a winter home for his invalid daughter, he was so favorably impressed by the climate here that he bought property and built a house. His friends followed him, built villas and gardens, and the present rendezvous of

MIDSUMMER ON THE BEACH AT CANNES

the wealthy was the result. To-day, Cannes has about twenty-five thousand inhabitants and entertains a large number of visitors. The harbor is not of importance, save for private yachts, and the city itself possesses few points of interest for the tourist; but it is a much favored resort and a favorite retreat for visitors, who enjoy brief excursions to the environs. Edward VII frequently visited Cannes, and a statue of the British monarch rises from the principal promenade.

Most popular are the Iles de Lérins, named Ste. Marguerite and St. Honorat. The legend is that in the saints' days, there was but one island. Honorat, a monk, came here because he wanted to leave the world. His sister followed him and established a convent at the other end of the island. According to the legend, they met frequently for conversation; but the brother desired isolation, so one morning, when he awakened, the island had divided into two, leaving a channel of water between them. After that, St. Honorat promised to pay his sister a visit once a year. The establishment of St. Honorat flourished mightily, and the island, like the other and larger one, Ste. Marguerite, has had a wonderful history.

The chief thing that attracts tourists to Ste. Marguerite is the fact that the "Man in the Iron Mask" was imprisoned in the fortress there. Just who he was, nobody seems to know of a certainty; but it is likely that he was a member of royalty, or at least a person of exalted station—possibly an heir to the throne—whom Louis XIV desired to keep in close confinement. Voltaire, who is said to have known more than he dared to publish, referred to him as "The Unknown."

"LA SOLITUDE," THE HOUSE AT HYERES IN WHICH STEVENSON
WROTE SOME OF HIS STORIES

Naturally, such a prisoner prompted many stories, and from them have been concocted many romantic hypotheses attempting to solve the mystery. One of these is that a child was born in the castle to a woman named Bompart, and that immediately after its birth it was sent away to Corsica and given into the charge of a person of quality, with instructions for a careful upbringing, as he came of *buona parte*. As the child was nameless, he was called Buonaparte and was an ancestor of Napoleon. The story declares that the infant was the son of the "Man in the Iron Mask," thus permitting Napoleon to derive from the French royal family. Another local legend, however, makes a more unlikely claim than this, because it is to the effect that the Masque de Fer was Louis XIV himself and that Le Roy Soleil was an impostor.

Hyères, splendidly situated on the slope of a hill, is three miles from the sea and sheltered from the winds of the north and east by the mountains. It is the oldest of the Mediterranean winter resorts; but it is likely to have a lower temperature than the towns lying farther east, so it has suffered somewhat in the competition for tourists during the cold months. One of the chief industries of the place is raising violets and early strawberries for the Paris trade. The town lies one-half mile from the railway station, and one passes through

A COAST SCENE NEAR
ST. RAPHAEL

THE NEEDLE, A PEAK NEAR CHAMONIX

ON THE WAY BACK TO THE RIVIERA

ST. RAPHAEL, WHERE NAPOLEON EMBARKED FOR HIS EXILE IN ELBA

an avenue of palms when entering the new town. Robert Louis Stevenson lived here one winter and wrote some of his best stories in Hyères. There are many attractive excursions in the vicinity.

St. Raphael repays a visit, altho it is a town of but five thousand inhabitants. It has become a favorite bathing place and winter resort, and while it is sheltered toward the east, it is exposed to the mistral. The church here has been called too massive for its size; but it is a reminder that the people fled to the church when the Saracens came, and that it was meant to serve as a fortified sanctuary. "As long as life does last," an early admirer declared, "the effort will be made to get back to the Boulevard Felix-Martin at St. Raphael."

XVIII CARCASSONNE

A QUIET VILLAGE BETWEEN CARCASSONNE AND THE PYRENEES

XVIII

CARCASSONNE

GOING westward from Marseilles, we stop for a day at Montpellier, a town with nearly eighty thousand inhabitants, yet one not included in the itinerary of the average American tourist. Montpellier has enjoyed a distinction for its medical college since the twelfth century, and to-day it has about five hundred students each year, some two hundred of whom are foreigners. The city's principal rendezvous is the promenade in the higher part of the town, known as the Peyron, which has a triumphal arch erected in honor of Louis XIV in 1691, and reliefs showing some of the events of his reign: the revocation of the Edict of Nantes, the union of the Atlantic and the Mediterranean by the Canal du Midi, and his military victories. There is also on the promenade a statue of Louis XIV, and at the end a reservoir, beyond which there is a view to the Pyrenees, and of the aqueduct that brings water to the city from the mountains. The Peyron ends in a double tier of arches more than half a mile long and seventy feet high. Below is the Jardin des Plantes, which is said to be the oldest in France, where many tropical plants flourish in the open air. The former bishop's palace is now occupied by the Faculty of Medicine, and the professor's chair in the amphitheater is from the Theater at Nimes. The Cathedral, founded in the fourteenth century, has been restored and enlarged.

GLIMPSED ALONG THE WAY

The principal sight of Montpellier is the Musée Fabre which contains one of the best provincial collections in France. The chief gallery has: "Portrait of a Senator," by Tintoretto; "The Holy Family," by Fra Bartolomeo; "Holy Family," by Giordano; "Grand Canal at Venice," by Canaletto; "Portrait of an Old Man," by Titian; "Head of the Virgin," by Guido Reni; "Portrait," by Rubens; "Marriage of Ste. Catherine," by Paolo Veronese; "Madonna and Child," by Van Dyck; and a copy of Michelangelo's "Last Judgment," dating from 1570. The so-called End Room contains, among others in a large collection, "The Infant Samuel," by Reynolds; "Village Fair," by Teniers the Younger; "Dutch Repast," by Jan Steen; and "Portrait of a Woman," by Maas. The upper gallery contains a "Portrait," by Courbet; "Evening on the Rhine," by Gustave Doré; "Michelangelo in his Studio," by Delacroix; "Arab Tents," by Fromentin; "Sea Piece," by Isabey; "The Good Samaritan," by Henner; and Fabre's "Portrait of Canova." The same building houses the Municipal Library, which has one hundred thousand volumes and ten thousand engravings.

Not far distant is Balaruc-les-Bains, with mineral waters that are popular with sufferers from chronic rheumatism, paralysis and scrofula.

Béziers, which has over fifty thousand inhabitants, is well

known to the world on account of its red wines and brandy. It was colonized by the Romans, and presumably was a town of importance long before that; but it suffered severely during the Albigensian wars, when in 1209 over twenty thousands of its citizens were massacred or burned, a catastrophe from which it never fully recovered. Its principal building is the Cathedral of St. Nazaire, which dates from the twelfth century. It is a Gothic structure, practically without ornament; but its windows retain their old glass and iron work. About one-half mile from the center of the town is the amphitheater, in which open-air performances are given in summer. There are also bull-fights in spring and summer.

Narbonne is situated five miles from the Mediterranean, with which it is connected by a canal. It does not appear to enjoy its former prosperity, altho it valiantly keeps up

THE NARBONNE GATE, ONE OF THE TWO ENTRANCES
TO CARCASSONNE

CARCASSONNE, THE DREAM CITY: JUST AS IT WAS EIGHT CENTURIES AGO

the struggle for industrial existence and carries on a trade in coopering and distilling. The old fortifications have been destroyed to make room for a new quarter that recently has come into existence. The town has little to attract visitors, as it retains but few remnants of its former grandeur. It is said to have been a flourishing town as early as the fifth century B. C., and it was colonized by the Romans fully a century before the beginning of the Christian era. Martial, in A. D. 95, speaks of it, and Sidonius Apollinaris refers to its theater, temple, capitol, baths, triumphal arches and other buildings, of which only ruined fragments remain.

Finally, we approach the place that has prompted anticipations since we reached the south of France. Carcassonne! There is music in the name, and there are few cities in the world that have been more admired or celebrated in more superlative praise by enthusiastic writers. "La Cité Glorieuse," sing the poets; "see Carcassonne before you die," say the people. Undoubtedly, it is the best existing example of a medieval fortified city in the world—a city better equipped than any other to give and to take the blows of battle as it was fought in the brave days of old. Nobody knows its origin. In 1928 it celebrated its two thousandth birthday with fitting pageantry, banquets and oratory; but that was an approximate estimate. In early times, Carcas, a eunuch at the court of Queen Esther, was said to have been its founder and to have given his name to the place. During the Middle Ages, it was the custom to give Æneas, son of Anchises, the honor. More scientific historians declare that the city was founded by the Phenicians; but whoever laid the first stones of the colossal pile, excavations prove that Carcassonne has been a human habitation from the earliest times. Pliny mentioned it as a stronghold, and it was occu-

WHAT THE MEDIEVAL ENEMY WAS UP AGAINST WHEN HE
TRIED TO STORM CARCASSONNE

pied in turn by the Romans, Visigoths, Saracens, and Franks; finally it came into the Kingdom of France in the thirteenth century.

As we view it from a distance, we see Carcassonne surrounded by an outer and an inner wall. The outer wall follows, more or less, the contour of the hill; and behind it rises, at what seems to be about twice its height, the inner wall, with numerous round towers, and beyond the huge mass, the turrets of the Cathedral of St. Nazaire and the towers of the château. Paul Wilstach, one of the city's enthusiastic admirers, has written:

"Heavy and massive and somber as this agglomeration of masonry undoubtedly is, still the lights and shadows on the vast broken surfaces, the square-scalloped tops of the walls, and the tapering conical tops of the towers looking like a flight of giant candle-snuffers, give it the lightness and grace of fancy. . . . The circumference of the outer wall is nearly one mile, that of the inner wall is about four-fifths of a mile. The space between the walls varies from twenty-three to twenty-six feet, and here the tournaments and jousts were held. The outer wall is interrupted at varying intervals by the bellying fronts of sixteen towers and barbicans, which sometimes rise one hundred feet above the ground. Above the inner wall rise thirty other towers. The fortified château contributes six additional towers to the entire picturesque cluster."

The place is divided into two sections: the old and the new cities. The old city is crowded behind its walls and towers; the new city, in which we arrive first, is spread out on a flat plain. "The old city has a past stretching indefi-

OLD CHURCH AND NEW HOTEL INSIDE THE WALLS OF CARCASSONNE

CARCASSONNE: WHERE YOU WALK OUT OF MODERN
INTO MEDIEVAL TIMES

nitely into the twilight of history. The new city is by comparison a civic upstart, for it had its beginning as late as
1247." Carcassonne prompts reflection, as we see, outlined
against the sky, those wonderful walls and towers which
have given Maxfield Parrish so much inspiration for his art.
The walls would quickly fall at the attack of heavy modern
guns, but they were considered impregnable in the days
when battles were fought with axes, spears, arrows, and bat-
tering-rams; when molten lead was poured upon the besiegers, and rocks were hurled upon the enemy from the tops
of towers. Here again, as so often in France, we look upon
a comparatively somber scene and think of the brilliant day
of color and romance—of the pomp of plumes, swords,
nobles and ladies in spectacular array.

The new city is laid out with the regularity of a checkerboard, has shady boulevards and several sights worth while, including its interesting market. But the chief object of our visit is the old town, which we reach by crossing the Pont Neuf over the Aude and entering the fortifications through the Porte de l'Aude. Once inside, it will be to our advantage, unless we have unlimited leisure, to accept the services of a local guide, who conducts us to the principal points of interest. Next to the fortifications themselves, the structure likely to attract our attention more than others is the Church of St. Nazaire, which was founded in the fifth century. Here are splendid stained-glass windows, various statues, tombs, and several ancient carvings. The present church was begun by that Louis of France who built the Sainte Chapelle in Paris and who was saint as well as king. On the exterior we note the gargoyles, which have been

WASH-DAY IN THE FRONT YARD OF MANY-TOWERED CARCASSONNE

[375]

compared to those on Notre Dame at Paris, and are said to number over four hundred—all with morbid, comic or sad faces, and as impressive as the masks worn by actors.

How long we remain at Carcassonne depends upon our time allowance and personal taste. One may spend hours or days wandering about the old town, visiting towers and other architectural relics, and in every excursion find much of interest. To the majority of American travelers, the visit to Carcassonne is an outstanding experience of a lifetime.

There is a new and excellent hotel here, built to harmonize with the ancient style of architecture. From its garden one obtains a wonderful view of the surrounding country. Its public and private rooms are all furnished to represent faithfully the days of long ago, a wonderful reminder of the walled city. There is but one Carcassonne. There can be no other place like it.

XIX IN THE SHADOW OF THE PYRENEES

LIFE IN THE FOOTHILLS OF THE PYRENEES

XIX

IN THE SHADOW OF THE PYRENEES

TOULOUSE, metropolis of the Pyrenees, was an
important town centuries before it was conquered
by the Romans. In fact, the ancient Tolosa had a
temple famous in antiquity for its treasures, which became
a large part of the rich booty of the invaders. The Pyrenees,
which form a wall between France and Spain and extend
from the Atlantic to the Mediterranean, seem to have been
almost as popular with travelers of the ancient world as they
are with modern trippers. In our day, as in Cæsar's, enthusiastic visitors avail themselves of the celebrated waters that
bubble from a thousand springs in the mountain chain and
bring prosperity to the inhabitants.

Toulouse has an air of prosperity; its commerce and industry, owing to its situation as the center of southern
France, are extensive. It has about one hundred and fifty
thousand inhabitants, who are thoroughly modern; but the
city has not a favorable reputation with tourists, especially
those who have been there in July and August. Those
months are uncomfortably hot, and at other times the high
winds at Toulouse are not agreeable. But it is a place to
see—one that should be visited, because it has its individ-
uality and is typical of the region.

Toulouse is old enough to have had its Sacred Lake. Pilgrims came to it from great distances, as to the lakes in Tibet,
and cast coins into the water, expecting favors from the

gods in return. But the lake has been drained; it was deprived of its water more than a century before the dawn of the Christian era—by a Roman consul who wanted the golden treasure in its muddy bottom. Then the pilgrims ceased to come, and now the inhabitants of the city live in houses built on the bed of the former lake, their foundations resting in a soil once considered holy. But modern tourists flock to Toulouse, regardless of the vanished lake; because the Romans erected fine buildings there, and established the atmosphere of art and culture which is still the city's pride. Shady avenues now follow the lines of the ancient walls of defense. Toulouse, unlike some of the cities in southern France, thinks of its present, as well as of its glorious past. Still, one should give a passing thought to the great events that have transpired here. After the fall of the Roman

A PROSPEROUS VALLEY IN THE PYRENEES

WHERE THE PYRENEES REACH THE CLOUDS

Empire, the city became the capital of the Visigoths. In 1562 it was the scene of a bitter struggle between the Roman Catholics and the Huguenots, in which four thousand of the latter perished. In 1814 the final battle of the Peninsular war took place here after Napoleon's abdication. The University of Toulouse, founded in 1229, next to that of Paris, is the oldest in France.

The sight most likely first to attract our attention in Toulouse is the Church of St. Sernin, one of the greatest of all Romanesque edifices of the kind and the chief monument of the city. It was begun at the end of the eleventh century and has been restored in modern times. The interior has large dimensions for a Romanesque structure. Under the choir is a crypt that contains relics of six Apostles, of St. Saturnin, of three of his successors, and of several other

saints. In the chapel of the north transept is a colossal
Byzantine figure of Jesus, and behind the choir are bas-reliefs
of the Holy Family attributed to Correggio. The carillon
plays the "Ave Maria de Lourdes" every hour.

The Cathedral of St. Etienne is an attractive if somewhat
inharmonious edifice. The interior seems rather small.
There are not the usual columns; the walls are hung with

A MOTOR ROAD IN THE PYRENEES

tapestry, and there is a general confusion of architectural
style, almost bewildering, but attractive. The Académie des
Jeux-Floraux of Toulouse is the oldest literary society in
Europe. Since its inception, the Floral Games have been held
annually in the month of May and writers contend for the
flowers of gold and silver. After the flowers have been blessed
at the church of Notre Dame de la Daurade, the members of
the society meet at the Hotel d'Assézat et de Clémence Isaure,
a handsome building of the sixteenth century, where the

amaranth of gold, the violet, eglantine, primrose and marigold of silver are presented to the winners of the contest. In the Place du Capitole, which is a market and the very center of the city's life, we find the inhabitants at rest and at play.

The Musée des Beaux-Arts is particularly rich in antiquities and pictures. It is housed in an old Augustine convent, and the ground floor has antique sculptures, altars, sarcophagi and inscriptions. In the picture gallery we observe particularly: Gérome's "Anacreon, Bacchus and Cupid," Canaletto's "Ponte di Rialto," Perugino's "Sts. John and Augustine," Van Dyck's "Achilles Detected by Ulysses," Réquier's "Carthusian Monastery," Henner's "Mary Magdalene," Corot's "Morning Star," and Vigée Le Brun's "Baronne de Crussol."

From Toulouse we go to Pau, which has a climate, particularly in winter, that has recommended it to all the world,

PAU AND ITS CASTLE SEEN ACROSS THE MOUNTAIN
STREAM THAT BEARS ITS NAME

[383]

THE CASTLE IN WHICH HENRI IV WAS BORN AT PAU

BEDROOM OF HENRI IV IN THE CASTLE AT PAU

making it a favorite rendez-vous for English - speaking visitors. It is a neat little city of thirty-five thousand inhabitants, with comparatively little of interest to travelers, yet one often hears it referred to as the "Little Paris of the South." Historically, the city owes its existence to the castle, erected in the tenth century; but to the loyal French it is the city whence came Henri IV, the knight of Navarre. His castle may be visited, and contains many sou-

PAU SEEN FROM THE CASTLE GATEWAY

venirs of general interest; for example, its Flemish and Gobelin tapestries. It was here that the ideas of the Reformation were received by sympathizers high in local power. When Calvin fled from his persecutors, he found a refuge in the Château of Pau; and when we are within its walls we recall that here Jeanne d'Albret, in her zeal for the Protestant cause, so far forgot her promise of immunity to six Catholic lords of Béarn as to permit them to be murdered. We visit the apartment in which she gave birth to the great Henri, the bed upon which the event transpired, and the tortoise-shell cradle in which he slept in his infancy. We hear that his mother chanted a hymn at his birth and her father showed the child to the crowd outside the château, shouting: "Behold, my ewe has given birth to a lion," whereupon he rubbed the infant's lips with garlic and gave him wine to drink. One hears much of Henri IV at Pau, but little of another king who was born

[385]

LOURDES ON THE OCCASION OF A GREAT RELIGIOUS FETE

here. He was a son of the family of Deu Pouey—which changed its name to Bernadotte—and he reigned over Norway and Sweden as Charles XIV.

One soon comes to appreciate the situation of Pau, which shows itself beautifully in the Promenade des Pyrénées and the panorama of the mountains in the vicinity. The promenade has been called a splendid platform from which to view the spectacle. One side is guarded by a great balustrade, and over this we view the hills, and beyond them the peaks against the azure blue of the horizon. Vineyards and orchards, among the best of France, are in the neighborhood.

The journey by train from Pau to Lourdes takes about one hour. Lourdes is the most notable Christian shrine in the world; nearly one million visitors arrive there annually to pay their devotions to the "Lady of Lourdes." The early history of the place is not easily distinguished from that of any of the other small towns of the Pyrenees. Like the others, it had its castle, which passed to the Romans, Saracens, Visigoths and the French. For a thousand years after the Moors surrendered it, Lourdes dozed in comparative obscurity until 1858, when a young shepherdess, Bernadette Soubirons, announced that she had seen apparitions of the Virgin Mary and received messages from her. Bernadette is responsible for the celebrity of modern Lourdes and for the thousands of visitors that arrive in the town every day in the year. She was the daughter of poor parents, and her occupation was guarding sheep. She could neither read nor write, nor even speak the French language, understanding only a Pyrenean dialect.

The official guide says that the apparitions took place between February eleventh and the sixteenth of July, 1858. On the first day she heard a rustling of the trees and shrubs, and saw the form of a "Lady" clad in a white robe tied with a blue sash. The apparition wore a white veil, and upon each of her feet was a golden rose. She made a sign to the shepherdess to approach, but this frightened the child, who recited the rosary, after which the form vanished.

The following Sunday, when the apparition returned, the shepherdess threw holy water toward her and said: "If you come from God, approach." The Lady descended through the niche that connects with the Grotto, and at her third appearance came near to Bernadette. "Do me the favor of coming here for fifteen days," she said; "I do not promise you happiness in this world, but in the other." At the fourth appearance, the Lady seemed pleased that the girl returned to the Grotto. At the fifth, she taught Bernadette a prayer, the words of which were never revealed. At the sixth, the

LOURDES IS BEAUTIFIED BY A CLEAR MOUNTAIN STREAM

Lady said: "Pray for sinners." During the seventh meeting, she told the shepherdess three secrets concerning herself, which the latter never revealed. At the eighth apparition, the Lady said only: "Penance, penance, penance." At the ninth, the girl heard: "Go, drink at the spring and wash yourself there," and at the tenth: "You will kiss the ground for sinners." The eleventh meeting was longer than the others, and the Lady said: "Go tell the priests, they must build a chapel here." At the time of the twelfth apparition, Bernadette descended to the Grotto slope, kissing the ground as she went. At the thirteenth, the Lady reproached Bernadette for using a rosary not her own. At the fourteenth, she said: "You will go to the priests and tell them to have a chapel built here and to come here in processions." There was a fifteenth apparition, concerning which the girl said little. At the time of the sixteenth, she asked the Lady's name and heard: "I am the Immaculate Conception." At the seventeenth apparition, Bernadette held her fingers in the flame of a candle, according to witnesses, and was not burned. There was an eighteenth apparition, and the series was at an end.

The miraculous cures had begun, and their fame was noised abroad. Paralytics walked and others were cured of eye disease. The pilgrims increased in number, year by year, until now they approximate a million annually. They arrive by train-loads—sometimes several trains are needed to carry one party. The Boulevard de la Grotte is about half a mile in length and leads from the railway station to the celebrated Grotto, where churches stand at the top and the foot of the cliff; and there is a promenade and a broad square that has statues of the Virgin and of St. Michael. The Grotto is about fifteen feet deep and fifteen feet wide. On a rock is

GROTTO OF THE VIRGIN AT LOURDES
Note the curtain of discarded crutches hanging at the left

a statue of the Virgin as the shepherdess saw her—in a white robe and blue sash. To the left is the miraculous spring, where pilgrims bathe. The Church of the Rosary, near by, is in Byzantine style; the Basilica, higher up, over the Grotto, is a richly ornamented edifice in Gothic style. All around are buildings for the accommodation of pilgrims—convents, hospices, asylums. All day long the pilgrims wait in line to join the solemn procession that enters the Grotto, at the left of which hang numerous crutches and sticks that have been thrown aside by cripples who arrived needing them and went away declaring that they were cured. Every day people bring fresh flowers and more candles. At the time of the French National Pilgrimage, the procession to the Grotto is endless, both day and night; there is a ceaseless "Pray for us" escaping from a thousand devout lips, and expectancy and hope on all faces—a scene that is often highly dramatic.

A medical bureau is maintained for the purpose of passing upon cases of pilgrims who claim to have been miraculously cured at the shrine. The official guide of Lourdes says that "more than a thousand doctors of all nationalities, all schools and all religions, succeed one another there each year with complete liberty. They examine and question the people who have been cured, exercising censorship over the witnesses and certificates, and make personal inquiries at will." It is noted, however, that the authorities at Lourdes use the word *cure*, as only a canonical inquiry can pronounce upon a *miracle*. It is claimed that there have been thirty miracles among about four thousand authenticated cures at Lourdes since Bernadette saw the apparitions at the Grotto.

An enjoyable excursion from Lourdes takes us up into the Pryenees to Cauterets, a town of only about two thousand inhabitants, yet equipped, it is said, to entertain ten thousand visitors at one time. There are numerous hotels and furnished apartments at Cauterets, and it is wise to make this a base for many short journeys into the neighborhood, for there are some popular spas near by.

From here we may easily extend our wanderings to the magnificent coliseum of nature known as the Cirque de Gavarnie, high up among the summits of the Pyrenees. The floor of the great box-canyon at Gavarnie, home of eternal snow, has an altitude of 5380 feet. Its walls rise much higher, and over one of these the waters from the melting snows come tumbling down over a precipice of more than a thousand feet—one of the highest waterfalls in Europe. No wonder the place is a favorite summer resort of French people from near and far! After describing Gavarnie at considerable length, Victor Hugo wrote: "Picture this to

PILGRIM CHURCH AT BETHARRAM, IN THE PYRENEES

yourself as I saw it—the black wall, the black towers, the dazzling snow, the blue sky; in a word, a thing of perfection—great beyond expression, serene even to sublimity!"

Bayonne is the metropolis of the Basque country, a distinctive section of France inhabited by a distinctive and interesting people. Nobody knows the exact origin of the Basques, who speak a language that is related to no other in this part of Europe. They do not mingle with other people; and they maintain their ancient customs and habits of life— a unique survival in the modern world.

Bayonne is a pretty town of about thirty thousand inhabitants, lying at the confluence of the Adour and the Nive. It is a city of bridges; and as bridges are always decorative, we think of this harbor as one of the much ornamented towns of the spectacular South of France, being reminded of Venice, altho Bayonne itself is wholly unlike the Queen of the Adriatic. The origin of the town, like that of the Basque people, is obscure. Probably it was the Lapurdum of the Romans; but it may have been in existence long before Roman times. During the Middle Ages its whaling fleet was famous, and one of the important days of its history was when, in 1565, an interview took place here between Charles IX of France and his sister Elizabeth, Queen of Spain, in the presence of their mother, Catherine de Medici, and the Duke of Alva, and the massacre of St. Bartholomew was planned.

The Cathedral was founded in the twelfth century, and the work continued until the sixteenth, when it was left unfinished. It is a notable edifice, probably the best of the Gothic structures in the Pyrenean country. I have been in Bayonne at various times in the last twenty years, and each time I have sought in vain through the Cathedral for the inscription in stone that amused Victor Hugo. During my latest visit I took up the search again; but inquiry of the attendant and a scrutiny of the various stones in the chapel led me to suspect that the inscription has passed from sight in the course of the numerous restorations. It carried the record that "the Royal Notary and the Messieurs of this chapter" gave "Pierre de Baraduc, Burgess and Man-at-Arms in the old castle of the town, the title and possession of this tomb in order that he and his may have the *enjoyment* thereof."

A pleasant excursion is to Cambo-les-Bains, where Edmond Rostand built a splendid villa, surrounded by a spacious garden. The author of "Cyrano de Bergerac" and "L'Aiglon" was born at Marseilles, but in the last years of his life he called the Pyrenees his home. Cambo-les-Bains

WHERE FASHION SPORTS ON THE SANDS OF BIARRITZ

is a favorite resort of the Basques, and large numbers of them gather here on St. John's Eve (June 23), when each tries to swallow the largest possible amount of the sulfur-spring water while the clock is striking twelve (midnight) in order to insure his good health for the next twelve months.

It is only about five miles from Bayonne to Biarritz, one of the most fashionable resorts in the world. Biarritz is a small city, but it has palatial accommodations for its guests, and, especially during September, is one of the most frequented bathing-places in Europe. The city stands on a line of cliffs that overlook the Bay of Biscay, and there is a fine beach with fantastically-shaped rocks, quaint coves and bays. The climate is free from extremes, so that while it is most popular with the Spaniards and French in summer, it is rapidly becoming a favorite rendezvous for English visitors in winter. Its Bar Basque and similar resorts, and its Casino (with much gambling), are gathering places for the smart set.

We go to the Place Bellevue, between the Casino and the Grand Hotel, obtaining there a splendid view of the sea and the coast-line. The Grande Plage extends one-half mile to Cap St. Martin, upon which there is a lighthouse. On a promontory stands the Villa Eugénie, erected by Napoleon III. There are many fine buildings, and the whole place has an air of elegance. Travelers find it convenient to cross the border into Spain from here, visiting San Sebastián, another celebrated resort facing the same waters.

Our journey through France should include a visit to Bordeaux, an important commercial center and the fourth largest city in the country. It lies upon the Garonne River, which, altho sixty miles from the Atlantic ocean, provides an excellent and safe harbor for the city. In fact, this har-

A MORE EXCLUSIVE RESORT AT BIARRITZ

bor, so far away from deep water, is one of the chief glories of the imposing city. The river, at Bordeaux, flows through a channel that makes almost a complete half-circle. The city stretches itself along this crescent and becomes the third seaport of France.

The buildings, streets and public institutions of this huge city are commensurate with its greatness. Its Grand Theater long has ranked as one of the finest in Europe. It is in the classical style, with a portico of twelve Corinthian columns, above which is a balustrade with colossal statues. The interior is sumptuous, in the old style. The Public Library contains a good collection of books and manuscripts, an example of its gems being the 1588 edition of Montaigne's "Essays" with the author's annotations. The Jardin Public is a popular and fine promenade, where band concerts are given. The ruins of the Amphitheater are also called the Palais Gallien, because the Emperor Gallienus is credited with building the structure. The old Cathedral of St. Seurin dates from the eleventh century and occupies the site of a much older sanctuary. The Hôtel de Ville was built to be the palace of the Prince-Cardinal de Rohan-Guéménée. The Cathedral of St. André is considered one of the finest Gothic churches in southern France. The principal portal is flanked by two towers, which support stone spires, and the sculptures in the tympanum represent "The Last Supper" and "The Ascension." There are several first-rate works of art in the interior. The bell tower, known as the Clocher Peyberland, was built in the fifteenth century; it has a gilded statue of the Virgin at the top, and a bell that weighs eleven tons.

The Musée Bonie has a collection of furniture, wood carving, weapons, porcelain, and a reproduction of Moorish rooms. The Church of St. Michel is Gothic and dates from the eighth century. Its portals are ornately decorated with religious sculptures. The bell-tower stands apart from the church. The soil of the cemetery, which is no longer used, had the property of preserving bodies interred in it, and about forty mummies are exhibited, standing against a wall. The Church of the Holy Cross was founded in the seventh century and has some interesting sculptures, altho nobody seems to be certain what they represent. The Museum of Painting and Sculpture has an interesting collection of old masters and modern works. And there is much else to interest the visitor, whose Bordeaux visit must depend upon the time he has to spend.

Before we turn our faces homeward or back toward Paris, let us take a good look at a handsome monument that stands

RIVER SCENE ALONG THE DORDOGNE

in the largest public square of Bordeaux. It is a memento of the French Revolution and was erected in honor of the deputies of the Gironde who dared at Paris, in the Convention, to raise their voices against the extreme radicals, Robespierre, Danton and Marat. It was the Gironde against the Montagnards. The fate of Louis XVI and Marie Antoinette already hung in the balance, and the deputies from the Gironde stood for moderate measures. It was the beginning of the furious partizan strife which ultimately destroyed the First Republic.

Vergniaud, leader of the staunch group from the region of Bordeaux, rose on the floor of the convention and shouted: "Death rather than crime!" To which Danton replied: "We will save liberty even at the expense of our good names!" The Montagnards were the stronger, and the king was exe-

[398]

cuted in what is now the Place de la Concorde. A hundred thousand peasants in La Vendée rose in revolt. The Girondins at Paris went on urging milder measures, but on June 2, 1793, the Commune surrounded the Convention with 80,000 soldiers and sixty cannons, and forced the arrest and imprisonment of twenty-seven moderates among its members. So the Gironde fell, and the Terror followed. Bordeaux revolted, and at Paris a young girl, Charlotte Corday, stabbed Marat to death in his bath to avenge the Girondins.

Wherever we go in France to-day we find marks of that historic crisis, such as this fine monument in the busy center of Bordeaux. Its granite shaft is surmounted by a gilded bronze statue of Liberty and is surrounded by groups of the leading Girondins and two fountains with figures of Concord

BRANTOME, IN THE PICTURESQUE DORDOGNE VALLEY

and the Republic seated in cars drawn by sea-horses. It is typical of the sturdy good sense of the main body of the French nation, which has enabled it to endure all the storms of the centuries.

INDEX

INDEX

INDEX

INDEX

[405]

171